POV Press
Books by Bethanne Kim

SURVIVAL SKILLS FOR ALL AGES #3

Simple Cooking for Families

BETHANNE KIM

Cover photo from the Carol M. Highsmith Collection at the Library of Congress, image #26271.

1. Cookbooks–Outdoor
2. Cookbooks–General

eBook ISBN: 978-1-942533-19-1
Paperback ISBN: 978-1-942533-19-1

Distributed by POV Press LLC
PO Box 399
Catharpin, VA 20143

Printed in the United States of America

Dedication

For all the moms who have to deal with kids and their food issues, even in a disaster. For the Survival Mom, who inspired this book. And of course, for my loving and supportive family.

Acknowledgments

One of the challenges all writers face is getting a great cover. My thanks to Kim Hill for her help on the cover, but true credit goes to the photographer and the artist who created the original mural: **The Lyda Hill Texas Collection of Photographs in Carol M. Highsmith's America Project, Library of Congress, Prints and Photographs Division.** They are the source for the cover image, a photo of a beach mural by Arturo Thomas (LOC #26271).

If you would like to support the work being done by Ms. Highsmith, artwork is available for purchase at:

photographs-america.hostedbywebstore.com/

Of course, if it wasn't for my own two crazy boys, I wouldn't have had the experience to know what I needed to write. So, my most sincere and deepest thanks to my two crazy boys, and my beloved and ever-supportive husband.

Table of Contents

TABLE OF CONTENTS

TABLE OF CONTENTS

TABLE OF CONTENTS

TABLE OF CONTENTS

TABLE OF CONTENTS

Introduction

I wrote for Lisa Bedford, the Survival Mom, for years. One day, looking through her posts, I was struck by all the recipes. I know there are already all kinds of cookbooks people can use in emergencies including solar cookbooks, canning cookbooks, campfire cookbooks, and so many more, but none of these really focused on feeding a family in an emergency. It's all well and good to say "if they are hungry enough, they'll eat it" about kids, but we all know that, if nothing else, we'll have a lot of tantrums and anger to deal with before they get to that point, and they may well have a stubborn streak that goes on for days. Instead of trying to convince a toddler that MREs are tasty, or a grade schooler that food beyond [insert food of the day here] exists, a better approach is making food in your regular life that can also be made in emergencies, with some small modifications. And so, the idea for this cookbook was born.

I'm from a long line of non-cooks. I don't have fond memories of anyone else in my family cooking or of big family meals. Cooking meals from scratch doesn't come naturally to me, although I have learned to be content doing it. Because of that, these are not complicated recipes. No advanced techniques are required. Your kids can probably make most of them, once they are old enough to be around stoves, knives, and other kitchen dangers.

INTRODUCTION

I lived in LA where earthquake (emergency) preparedness is encouraged by pretty much everyone. I'm also a life-long Scout, so I've done campfire cooking. And I have a serious gadget issue. (If they had Gadget Lovers Anonymous, I might not ever get a one month chip for making it one month without buying a new gadget.) With all that combined, I have everything I need to make all these recipes without electricity. The primary ones I use are a whisk, pastry blender, stick blender, and mortar and pestle. I also use my blender a fair amount, but I don't even own an electric mixer now that I have my stick blender.

There are two cookbooks in this book series. I have worked to make them complimentary with few duplicate recipes. There are a few that are in both cookbooks but with entirely different recipes (cheesecake, for example). There are others where the two books have different versions of a popular food (teriyaki chicken wings and parmesan chicken wings).

Simple Cooking for Families provides recipes for basic foods many of us (myself included) would never even think about making at home such as brown sugar, crackers, vanilla wafers, and more. It also includes information on off-grid cooking tools, long-term storage food, and a chapter on how to modify recipes.

Simple Cooking for Allergies: Oral Allergy Syndrome and Low Histamine Food was written for people with allergy issues, especially seasonal allergies, but my tween convinced me it should be in this series. In an emergency, it's easy to be subjected to more histamines while also having less anti-histamines available, and food can also contain histamines, making allergy problems even worse. *Simple Cooking for Allergies* explains how to make meals lower histamine.

Because of my personal allergy issues, I didn't do one of the most basic things cookbook writers do: I haven't exactly followed all these recipes because I can't eat many spices but I don't think that impacts the actual cooking. There are a few seasoning mixes (like Ranch Mix) that are too good to not include, but that my allergies prevent me from eating at all. In spite of the admitted blandness, my family has enjoyed these recipes as part of our everyday diet

In an emergency, most of the recipes in this book can simply be made on a camp stove or fire. If you use a camp stove, there shouldn't be many changes. If you make them on a camp fire, the times will definitely change but there are far too many variables that affect the temperature of the fire and how it will heat the food for me to safely and accurately give specific instructions. If you make one of those meals over a campfire, watch it to see how long it takes to boil, simmer, brown, sauté, or whatever else the recipe describes. Other recipes, particularly baked goods, are best made using a solar cooker. Again, some solar cookers are more efficient than others. I use the Sun Oven®, which is harder to transport than some other solar cookers but also gets to 400°F +. That's pretty amazing for a solar cooker.

There are a lot of recipes in here that I really love. If you see that a lot in this book, it's not because I'm getting super excited about each recipe. It's because I choose recipes I and my family love to include in my cookbooks, and because I sought out "comfort foods" from around the world. This way, we have food we love to eat and we get to share our favorites with other people who will hopefully enjoy them the way we do.

Good luck and happy eating!

Bethanne Kim

1. Cooking Tools and Methods

I am a big fan of not using electric appliances for cooking. I haven't a clue why, but I have used a pastry blender and whisk ever since I can remember, even though my mom is a firm user of her stand mixer. As my cooking skills and preparedness knowledge have expanded, I have added more and more non-electric appliances, including an egg beater, a hand-powered mini-food processor, and a non-powered slow cooker. We even have a hand-powered coffee grinder and cold brew system so no one will have to go without coffee in an emergency. My blender and stick blender are the primary electric appliances I use.

Some of off-grid tools are beloved and well-known, such as the Dutch oven and solar oven, but there are many more off-grid and hand appliances available, if you know what to look for. Most can be used in regular daily life, no disaster needed. I've been known to pound out my frustrations on dough using a pastry blender and my husband finds cold-brew coffee better tasting than "regular" brewed. In an emergency, using hand powered tools is a clear win.

The Resources section of this chapter lists my top picks for non-electric appliances so you don't have to spend your time looking for a good quality one. I used a mediocre quality pastry blender for *20 years* before getting a restaurant-quality one, and woe onto anyone who messes with my pastry blender because I've never seen one like it again. It was *so* worth the $20 I spent on it! The beauty of many non-electric kitchen gadgets is that top-quality ones are quite inexpensive.

COOKING TOOLS AND METHODS

A decent electric mixer is easily two or three times as much as a top quality whisk, pastry blender, mini-food processor, and egg beater. A top quality mixer is much more.

Camp Fires

Camp stoves and camp fires (or fires in a fireplace) are probably the main cooking methods most people will use if there is no power, depending on where they live. Campfires are almost certainly the oldest way to cook food, and they still work. The simplest methods of putting something on a stick (or metal skewer) and heating it in a pot over the fire both still work, and they are the simplest. Boiling in a pot over a fire is particularly easy.

Dutch ovens are another classic method of campfire cooking, although ones designed for outdoor use normally use charcoal, not just a fire. Dutch ovens open a lot more options, including baked goods like apple crisp.

If you have a working fireplace in your home, you can attach a specially designed hook to the wall to keep a kettle above the fire and make cooking inside easier.

Camp Stoves/Grill

If you have a camp stove, it's a simple matter to move food from a stovetop to a camp stove with little to no change in preparation, especially if you have a propane powered grill. There are seemingly infinite choices with a wide variety of fuels, capacity, styles and sizes. Backpacking and other smaller types of camp stoves will require more modification but there are far too many variations to go into that here.

Cast Iron

Cast iron lasts forever, with a small bit of care, and is healthy for you since the food absorbs trace amounts of iron that your body needs while cooking. The only made-in-America, widely-available, quality brand still being produced it Lodge. If you are buying new, buy Lodge. It's really that simple.

When you clean it, never, EVER use soap on your cast iron. Ever. If you do, you will have to re-season the whole thing after you remove the rust with fine steel wool, starting from scratch for the seasoning, and you really don't want to have to do that. It's not hard, but it is a bit stinky and takes time. Always, always, always dry cast iron completely. You can dry it with a tea towel, just like anything else, but use care to dry it completely to prevent rust. If you put it on a burner (gas or electric) on low for a few minutes, it should dry completely.

Coffee Pot & Bean Grinder

It's a rare home that doesn't have a coffee pot and many also have a coffee bean grinder but most of them require electricity. What happens when the power goes out? The horror of no coffee is something most wouldn't want to contemplate. In addition to a camping or other power-free coffee pot (like pour over styles), you will really want to have a bean grinder. Even if you don't normally grind your own beans, in a longer-term situation, it could be the difference between a fresh cup to bring you joy and a cup of instant coffee, and that goes for the people around you, too. Don't forget filters.

Cooking Spray

Skip the cooking spray and grease pans the old-fashioned way. Use a finger-full of butter, oil, or lard to coat the surface. Read the list of ingredients for cooking spray, then the ingredients in your favorite butter or oil to see how even lard is healthier. If you put a small piece of cling wrap around your fingers, you can simply scoop out what you need without contaminating what is still in the container. This makes it easy to keep your hands clean and grease-free while you grease the cooking surface.

I now prefer butter to cooking spray because it makes clean-up easier. Cooking spray often leaves a sticky brown residue on the edges of pans that simply isn't there with more traditional, old-school methods.

Dutch Oven (Cast Iron)

There are two kinds in modern use, but Dutch ovens have been popular for over 300 years. The more recent style is has a rounded lid and flat bottom, making it easy to use in an oven or on a stove-top. The older type is designed for use with charcoal. It has legs for standing in the fire and a flat lid with a rim to stack charcoal on. If you have both kinds, it is even easier to use every-day recipes in an emergency. All you do is switch from cooking on a stove to a fire.

It is important to get a good, solid lid lifter for an outdoor, charcoal heated Dutch oven. If you don't, it is easier to let ash and coals from on top of the oven slip into your food when you remove the lid. A sturdy lid lifter and a steady hand can prevent that.

Egg Beater

Egg beaters are like a small, hand-powered mixer. They can't handle a thick dough, but if you need to "beat egg whites to a peak", you'll get there much faster with this than with a whisk. Egg beaters are primarily used with liquids, but I freely admit that this is one place where an electric beater comes in handy.

Food Processor

This is a fast way to chop and blend food and they come in a variety of sizes. The small size is perfect for small amounts, such as spices or some sauces. Salsa maxes completely fills the container for our small one. In addition to standard electric versions, hand-powered food processors are available.

Stand mixers sometimes have food processor attachments and can, obviously, handle larger amounts. Stand mixers may also have meat grinding or other useful attachments available.

Grills

My favorite grill is the Cobb Grill®. It's designed for tailgating and can actually be transported even while it's cooking. But the choices are virtually infinite. One of the first choices you need to make is whether you want to use charcoal or not. Determining your preferred fuel will help narrow your search, as will deciding if you want a portable grill or more of a backyard barbeque grill–or both.

Meat Grinder

There are tons of options including mixer attachments, hand-powered, and electric. This is definitely not a place to skimp because if you use one, it will have to work hard and it's not hard to imagine a dangerous situation arising from a malfunctioning meat grinder. Clearly, hand powered will still work even without power, making them a good apocalypse purchase but electric is easier in regular life.

Mortar and Pestle

I find myself continually amazed by how often I've been using my mortar and pestle to crush things when I'm cooking. Roasted flax seeds, graham crackers and cookies for crusts, bread for bread crumbs…. Given that the mortar and pestle is well over 10,000 years old (not a typo–the oldest one found is nearly 35,000 years old), it's no surprise that it is well-suited to use in an emergency. However, most are stone and very heavy so you really wouldn't want to carry one around.

If you don't have (or want) one, many times you can simply put the food in a closed plastic bag and crush it with a rolling pin. I prefer a mortar and pestle because the sharp edges of the crushed food can make tiny holes in the bag, potentially making a mess, and because in an emergency, you may not have any sealable plastic bags at all, so I recommend keeping a mortar and pestle on hand.

If you have a stone mortar and pestle and find odors and stains sticking to it, grind a cup or so of white rice, then rinse with warm water (no soap) and dry. Repeat if necessary. Softer stones may absorb

COOKING TOOLS AND METHODS

some of the taste from soap, so try to stick with just warm water and soap to clean it.

Foodal.com has a great post "How to Choose and Use the Best Mortar and Pestle Set" with some outstanding tips on exactly that, including pros and cons of stone, wood, and clay/porcelain sets. While none of the online reviews mention it, Ikea® has a great looking set that I plan to buy next time I go to an Ikea.

Pastry Blender

Pastry blenders are designed to cut pats of cold butter or lard into dry ingredients and help create a lighter, airier final produce. Because of that, don't melt butter or put in giant chunks of butter. Either can present challenges. I use my pastry blender baking cookies and anything with thicker dough. If the final step of a recipe is to "form it" into a ball or any other shape or roll it out, it's probably a good candidate for a pastry blender, but not a whisk.

Pie Iron

A pie iron is hinged with a long handle and designed to hold one or more sandwiches while you cook them over a campfire or other open flame. I think of the end results as something of a simple, old-school panini.

Caution! Pie-irons heat up quickly, so use the wooden handles and keep leather gloves available.

Slow Cooker/Wonderbag™

"Crock Pot®" is actually a trademarked name, although it's often used to refer to any slow cooker. Slow cooker is the generic name that encompasses all similar cookers, including the off-grid "Wonderbag." These cook food at a lower temperature for a longer time, making them a great way to prepare meals ahead of time. Since recipes can be started at night and left to cook while you sleep or in the morning and left to cook while you are at work, etc., they are great for busy families. You can even bake bread and desserts in them. No joke!

When you buy a Wonderbag, you are literally buying an insulated bag, and it takes a fair amount of shelf space. This isn't something you are likely to want in a tiny home but I think it's great for pot lucks, picnics, tailgating, and things like that. In addition to slow cooker favorites like stew, the Wonderbag can make yogurt and dulce de leche (caramel). It's really a very simple tool but I'm a huge fan of simple tools because there are fewer ways for them to fail.

Solar Cooker/Oven

The basic principal is that there is a reflector that reflects sunlight back into a box to heat it up and cook/bake your food. The inside heats up, just like a car on a summer day, and the built-up heat cooks the food, as long as the lid remains tightly latched.

Solar cookers are versatile but clearly are limited to times when the sun is out. Generally, unless the solar cooker casts a strong shadow when placed outdoors, there isn't enough sunlight to cook the food. As you move closer to the north and south poles, the weaker rays of the winter sun affect cooking time. This is another reason why it takes things longer to cook in the winter at my house.

It's easy to find DIY plans online if you want to make your own and there are a variety of brands and styles you can buy online that should last for years. Because solar cookers should be turned periodically as the sun moves to ensure the inside doesn't become shaded as the day progresses, most solar ovens are designed to be at least somewhat portable. I have seen pictures of a few large, permanent ones for whole villages!

There are several professional models of solar cookers that work quite well. I have a Sun Oven, which is easy to take outside from the house and gets over 400°F, which is extremely hot for a solar oven, but it wouldn't be portable on a camping trip. There are others that are designed for camping but they don't necessarily get as hot or have as large a cooking space. Look at the options and think about whether you will keep it at the house, carry it in a backpack, or somewhere in between.

WAPI (Water Pasteurization Indicator)

Clean drinking (potable) water is one of the most basic human needs. Most of us are spoiled by having it come out of taps but that is dependent on modern infrastructure. In an emergency, that might not be available. Boiling it is clearly one way to purify it, tablets and purification tools are good solutions as well. I like WAPIs because they are good virtually indefinitely, and very inexpensive.

Pasteurization makes food (milk, water, even eggs) safe to consume at a lower temperature than boiling. Boiling takes more time and uses more fuel. The WAPI is a small cylinder with a small amount of wax in it. When the water reaches pasteurization temperature, the wax melts to indicate that.

Whisks

Whisks can be used instead of an electric mixer for thinner consistency batters, typically thicker than you would use an egg beater for and thinner than you would use a pastry blender. If the final step of the recipe is to "pour" the batter, it's probably a good candidate for whisking. There are a surprising variety of sizes and styles of whisks for specific uses, but a basic teardrop shaped whisk works for most home cooking needs.

Rubberized or silicone coatings are nice if you have an anti-stick coating that could be scratched or damaged by a metal whisk, but the coating can be damaged over time so they may not last as long. We have a small silicone-coated whisk to mix scrambled eggs in the pan, a larger metal one that is my favorite, and an itty bitty one sometimes used to mix ingredients in the measuring cup.

Resources

Oxo has well-reviewed small kitchen gadgets of all kinds, including these. I particularly like their measuring cups. If you don't have their

Tablespoon and Ounce liquid measuring cups, you should buy one. Right now. The rest of these are mostly specific recommendations (Cobb Grill), but there are a few items where it's hard to go wrong, like a mortar and pestle. There are also a lot of good options for thermometers.

Non-electric appliances

- Cast iron pans, including Dutch ovens
- Cobb Grill
- Coffee pot
- Coffee grinder (Wheroamaz Manual Coffee Grinder)
- Egg beater (Norpro Classic)
- Mortar and pestle
- Pastry blender (Winco 5 Blade)
- Sun Oven (solar cooker)
- Thermometers: candy (also used when frying), frothing (for drinks), meat, and refrigerator (if power goes out, you can check if the temperature is still safe)
- Whisk (Ouddy Balloon Silicone, Winco Piano Wire Whip)
- Wonderbag (slow cooker)

2. Long Term Storage Food

If you are planning for an emergency, there is no way around the need for long term storage food for everyone in your family, including pets. If anyone has or develops special dietary needs including allergies, check your food stores to be sure their needs are accommodated. The bare minimum recommended amount of food storage for a long-term emergency is two weeks with some people having up to a year of food for themselves and their family. That is *a lot* of food to store.

There are several categories of food commonly used for long-term storage, including canned, dehydrated, freeze dried, and grains. There are also some specialized foods like TVP (Textured Vegetable Protein) and a few foods that effectively don't expire, such as salt, honey, and baking soda. The recipes in this book use a wide variety of them and you should keep a variety for your family.

Canning

When a recipe uses meat, chicken, produce, marinara, or salsa, and you're wondering what a shelf-stable option might be, remember that these can all be home canned. Home canned goods are healthier than comparable manufactured goods. You control what goes—and doesn't go—into them. You don't like onions? Good luck finding a manufactured salsa without them, but if you make your own, that problem is solved. The same goes for virtually every other food.

Most people who store food long-term end up doing some home canning since it's such an effective way to preserve foods. There are many good resources that teach canning and have canning recipes so they aren't included in this book. Studies have shown some canned food, especially commercially canned, can stay safe to eat for decades, although the taste doesn't stay good. Nonetheless, canning is a good way to store some of your family's favorites that might be hard to make or find in an emergency, and it's arguably the best way to store excess fruit and vegetables.

Canned store-bought favorites, such as soup, is a good way to augment your deep pantry with everyday favorites you can eat in an emergency.

Dehydrated Foods

Dehydrated food has had the water taken out of it using relatively low levels of heat (150-200°F or so versus 350°F+ to cook) to help it stay safe to eat for longer. You normally put the water back (rehydrate it) before eating, although some things (jerky, fruit leather) are eaten dehydrated. The food pieces shrink to a fraction of their original size and weight to make carrying and storage easier. They are rehydrated before being used in most recipes, although rehydration can be part of the cooking process. Once rehydrated, they look similar to fresh. One of my go-to dehydrated items is buttermilk.

It might surprise a lot of people, but most of us have eaten dehydrated food because most of us have, at some point, eaten Kraft Mac 'n' Cheese, which includes dehydrated cheese, and box-mix potatoes or stuffing. Why do you think they fluff up so much when you add water or milk? Because they are dehydrated! Raisins are another dehydrated food. You can buy a dehydrator and dehydrate your own food. That's what I do when I realize I'm really not going to use carrots or other veggies I they go bad.

Some things are best left to the professionals. Milk is a prime example of that, and it is available in varieties other than cow milk, such as goat's milk. The items in this list should be professionally processed and all are the ingredients to make other foods, not complete meals in and of themselves.

Butter / Margarine

Eggs

Egg Whites

Milk (Cow)

Milk (Goat)

Peanut Butter

Potatoes (Mashed)

Sour Cream

Whipped Dessert Topping

Home-dehydrated foods have a far shorter shelf life than store-bought ones. One year is generally safe, beyond that mold and other hazards may start to develop. Home dehydrating is a great way to give yourself some extra time to use perishable items, to make it easier to transport them (such as for camping), and to make treats such as jerky and fruit leather. Most homes simply don't have the equipment to dehydrated, process, and store food safely for genuinely long-term storage.

Dehydrated (dried) beans are incredibly cheap and easy to find. There is really no reason to go to the effort to do this at home unless you grew a bumper crop of beans in your yard, and even then canning may be a better use of your time since home-canning methods are more reliable and well-studied over the long term.

Freeze Dried Food

Freeze dried foods look nearly identical to fresh because the freeze drying process retains the size, shape, and color of the food. Freeze dried raspberries and blackberries are almost identical to their fresh counterparts and are commonly used in desserts and smoothies, but they can be easily crushed into dust.

When food is freeze-dried, it is flash-frozen (frozen super quickly so ice crystals don't form), the moisture removed, and packaged. It is much less temperature-sensitive than most foods, is extremely light-weight, and can be returned to its original state just by adding boiling water, even decades later. If you want to try some but don't want to spend a lot of money, the toddler section of some big box stores carries freeze dried fruits and berries for tiny tots. For just a few dollars, at a store you probably already frequent, you can give it a try. I snack on these without rehydrating the crunchy little morsels of sweetness!

It's not something most people think about, but freeze dried meat can actually be a cost-effective way to stretch your budget.

Foods with Indefinite Shelf Life

As with so many things, storage is important. In an airtight container away from light, moisture, and heat, each of these should last for years or even decades. Salt and vinegar, in particular, are used to preserve other foods, so it makes sense that they would at least take a long time to expire. Many of these contain high levels of sugar or salt.

Baking soda
Bouillon cubes (keeping them dry is very important)
Coconut oil
Corn starch
Corn syrup
Cream of tartar
Honey
Maple syrup*
Popcorn kernals
Rice (white, not brown)
Salt
Soy sauce*
Sugar (brown and white)

Vanilla extract, pure (not imitation)

Vinegar

*Once opened, these should be refrigerated but will stay good for years after opening, as long as they are kept cool.

Just because it's still edible doesn't mean time doesn't impact these foods. Cream of tartar and baking soda can lose some of their effectiveness. Honey crystallizes over time and sugar can harden and clump. Heating honey helps it reconstitute and become easy to work with again. Sugar clumps can also be softened and used again. Maple syrup may get some "harmless" surface mold. Skimmed it off and the rest of the syrup should still be fine to eat. In addition to these specific examples, food may simply look different, and less appetizing, as it gets old but that doesn't necessarily make it unsafe.

Salt and Vinegar: Nature's Preservatives

Since the early 20th century, most American table salt has had iodine added. This was originally done because food from some areas didn't have enough iodine because of the soil properties. This led to people getting goiters and thyroid problems, as well as to problems during pregnancy. Adding iodine to table salt, something almost everyone uses, has had wide-spread health benefits. Today, with food sourced from all over the world, it may not be necessary any more, but in a long-term emergency situation, it could be a blessing to have salt with added iodine, depending on where you live. Salt is clearly marked as having added iodine, if it does, and it is very easy to get salt that does not have added iodine, if you prefer.

Salt has many uses beyond sneaking iodine into our diet. Seasoning is the main use today, but all salt is not the same. The best salts for your body have color. It could be pink (Himalayan), or gray (Celtic), or something else, but white isn't optimal for the best nutrition. Pure white salt has almost always been heavily processed, even bleached. If you think about it, snow is one of only a few things in nature that are snow-white. Most things only become pure white after bleaching or heavy processing of some sort, and salt is no exception. Processing also removes naturally occurring trace mineral elements your body needs. SheKnows.com has a great post on "different kinds of salt" that discusses which are best for cooking different foods.

Historically, salt was used to preserve foods. This cookbook has a recipe for brined turkey, and brining is a way of preserving meat with salt. Like salt, vinegar has historically been used to preserve foods and there are more kinds of it than most people realize. Varieties include white, rice wine, red wine, apple cider (with/without the mother), balsamic, and many more, each with a slightly unique taste. White vinegar is true champ for longevity, but apple cider vinegar with the mother (least longevity) is widely considered the healthiest.

Vinegar is also used as a preservative, most commonly in pickling food. Pickled food goes far beyond the obvious "pickles" to include things like sauerkraut and pickled eggs. Pickled things are frequently canned, making canning books a great place to look for tips on pickling.

TVP: Textured Vegetable Protein

TVP is a dehydrated soy product used to replace or stretch meat (and your hard-earned dollars) in long-term storage meals. It comes in a variety of flavors including unflavored, sausage, chicken, beef, taco, ham, and bacon. Personally, I use it in Sloppy Joes even without an emergency. Everything else has so much flavor that it's a great place to try even unflavored TVP. It perfect when I haven't gotten to the grocery store recently.

It sounds incredibly unappetizing and looks almost as uninspiring, there is no denying that, but you don't need to tell your family you are serving them TVP until after they've enjoyed it, if ever. It will never become the main source of protein for most families but it is great to keep on hand for times you don't have fresh meat on hand to make tacos, lasagna, chili, or whatever else is on the menu.

3. Substitutions

Even if it isn't an emergency, we all run out of things (or can't find them) sometimes. In an emergency? Doubly and triply so! Here are some common ingredients you may not have on hand or could run out of in an emergency. These are possible substitutions for them, but you can do some research online to see if there is something out there that works better for your family. I choose the ones that seem the easiest for most people.

This is one area where I haven't tried all the options listed because my allergies are an issue, but it's good to have choices in an emergency. There are also recipes for some of these in Chapter 5.

Buttermilk

- Soured milk.
- Add buttermilk powder to regular milk.
- Combine equal parts sour cream and water.
- Combine ¼ c. water or milk with ¾ c. plain yogurt to replace 1 c. buttermilk.
- Add 1¾ tsp. cream of tartar to 1 c. milk.
- Add 1 Tbsp. lemon juice or white vinegar to 1 c. milk and let sit for 5 minutes; when tiny curdles start to form, it's ready to use.
- Whey, especially sweet whey (when you don't use vinegar or lemon juice in the process)

Cream Cheese

These are slightly less sweet than cream cheese so you may need to add some honey or another sweetener, to taste.

- Blend cottage cheese until smooth in a blender or food processor to use in place of cream cheese.
- Ricotta and yogurt (plain or Greek), strained in cheese-cloth overnight to reduce the liquid content for best results.
- Combine 4oz. of ricotta and 4 oz. of yogurt to equal 8 oz. of cream cheese.

Gelatin

I've always been a bit grossed out whenever I read what gelatin is made of. I finally went in search of a substitute and found the plant-based Asian staple agar agar. It reportedly has a lot of health benefits, especially compared to gelatin, but it also has the benefit of being shelf-stable and melting at a much higher temperature than gelatin. This means your jello won't melt as fast in the summer heat!

Agar agar can be found in Asian markets or ordered online. It is more expensive than gelatin but a little bit goes a long way. Generally, 1 tsp. of agar agar powder, 1 Tbsp. agar agar flakes, or ⅓ c. agar strands (cut in 1" pieces) is added to 1⅓ c. water for a firm jelly, but you can vary the amount of water based on the desired consistency.

Heavy Cream

I've been very surprised by how many recipes use heavy cream.

- Melt ⅓ c. butter and let it cool but not to the point of congealing. Add it to ⅔ c. whole milk* and whisk until thickened.
- Combine 2 Tbsp. cornstarch OR unflavored gelatin and 1 c. skim milk. Whisk 3-4 minutes, until the mixture thickens.
- Blend equal amounts of unflavored soy milk and tofu until the mixture is smooth for a vegetarian option.

- For a vegetarian option, blend equal amounts of cottage cheese and dehydrated milk or skim milk until the mixture is smooth. A food processor would probably make this much easier.
- Use ½ c. cream cheese (preferably low fat) for every 1 c. of heavy cream.

*If you use low-fat milk, add 1 Tbsp. flour.

Original Source: TheDailyNutrition.com (Make Heavy Whipping Cream)

Eggs

Dehydrated or powdered eggs definitely should be included in your deep pantry even if you have chickens. You can also pasteurize eggs (page 109) to reduce the chances of salmonella.

Lemon (Fresh)

In place of 1 fresh lemon, use 2 Tbsp. juice or 1 Tbsp. zest.

Meat

The easiest substitution is canned meat for fresh. If you need ground meet, you can shred canned meat with a cheese grater. You can also use TVP, described in Chapter 2.

Milk

Dehydrated or powdered milk is readily available and comes in a wide variety including goat milk, not just cow milk.

Sour Cream

- Dehydrated sour cream.
- Yogurt, plain or Greek.
- Buttermilk can be used in some baked goods but is far more liquid and may change the consistency; combine ¾ c. buttermilk or sour milk with ⅓ c. soft butter.
- Milk (evaporated, dehydrated, or fresh) works, too. Combine 1 c. whole milk and 1 Tbsp. lemon juice, or

blend ⅔ c. dehydrated milk, ¾ c. water, and 1 tsp. lemon juice or vinegar.

Yogurt

- Sour cream.
- Buttermilk.
- Cottage cheese, blended smooth (if desired).
- Coconut cream: Refrigerate a can of full-fat coconut milk to allow the cream to rise to the top. Skim off the cream and use it in place of yogurt.
- Pureed tofu.
- Whey, especially sweet whey (when you don't use vinegar or lemon juice in the process)

Xanthum Gum

- Corn starch or unflavored gelatin. Use the same amount of either you would use of xanthum gum.
- Chia seeds–they don't even need ground!
- With flax seeds, use the same weight of ground flax as the recipe calls for xanthum gum. Create a slurry by adding twice the amount of hot boiling water.

4. Grocery Store Staples

This cookbook has lots of long-term storage foods but not all our everyday basics can be stored long-term, like crackers. Other recipes in here are for pantry basics that you may run out of, like baking powder. Baking powder has a fairly short shelf life. The ingredients used to make it have a shelf life measured in decades.

I didn't expect to ever need to make brown sugar. Then, one afternoon, my son went to a girl's house to make cookies. The list of ingredients for him to bring included brown sugar and I sent him with my whole container. Naturally, I decided to make something that needed brown sugar a half hour after he left. Rather than open a new container, I made a cup of homemade brown sugar. Problem solved! And it wasn't even an actual emergency.

Crackers are a hugely popular snack, especially with little kids, and no emergency will change that. It might, however, make it hard to get favorites from the store. The first two recipes are the most important. Why? Because small children may lose their minds if they can't have Goldfish® or Cheez Its®, so it's good to be able to make them. Making them is also healthier and saves some money.

NOTE: With any kind of crackers, rolling them paper-thin is super important. If you think you've gotten them too thin, they are probably just about right. If you think they might be a little too thick, roll them thinner. Also, I highly recommend the website CakeWhiz.com. They have a *ton* of recipes for ultra-basics like brown sugar and lemon curd.

Baking Powder

Baking *soda* has a really, *really* long shelf-life. Baking *powder* does not. Little known fact: You can make baking powder by combining baking soda and cream of tartar, which is relatively cheap purchased in bulk (1 lb.+) online compared to the small containers at the grocery store. Adding corn starch helps it last longer. It is an insanely simple and easy recipe.

> 1 tsp. baking soda
>
> 2 tsp. Cream of tartar
>
> 1 tsp. corn starch (if you plan on storing it)

Thoroughly mix one part baking soda and two parts cream of tartar. If you need to store it, add one part corn starch and keep it in the refrigerator.

Mix 1 tsp. baking soda + 2 tsp. cream of tartar, and add 1 tsp. of cornstarch for storage, or 2 c. baking soda + 4 c. cream of tartar, and 2 c. corn starch if you need a really big batch. Whatever amount you need, you need twice as much cream of tartar as you do baking soda and corn starch.

DoesItGoBad.com recommends stirring ½ tsp. cream of tartar into ½ c. warm water, then add a pinch of baking soda to test if it's still good. If it foams, it's still usable for baking.

Bread Crumbs

My kids go through loaves of bread super-fast–until they don't. Then the loaves just set there until they go bad. This is a way to keep them from being a waste.

> Bread slices

Preheat oven to 200°F. Put slices of bread in the oven for 20-40 minutes, depending on how dry (stale) the bread already is. When it is

GROCERY STORE STAPLES

golden brown and dry, remove it from the tray. Either put it in a plastic bag and crush it with a rolling pin, or crush it with a mortar and pestle. Depending on the size and thickness, one slice of bread should yield about ⅓ c. of bread crumbs, but that is just an estimate.

Substitutes:

- Cereal: bran cereal, Cheerios®/rice flake cereal (equal amounts), cornflakes, Wheaties®, corn or rice Chex®
- Panko (Japanese bread crumbs)
- Quick oats (in meatballs and hamburgers)
- Cornstarch or parmesan cheese (for coating patties or chicken before frying)
- Pretzels, potato chips, tortilla chips, frosted flakes, croutons, etc.

Brown Sugar (Light or Dark)

Yes, brown sugar *is* something you can make, and it's one of the few recipes that is simpler and faster than baking powder. When I made this, it took about two minutes, including measuring the ingredients. You can use a mixer, but I started mixing this with a spoon and finished using my hands, it's that easy to do.

1 c. sugar

1-1½ Tbsp. (to taste) unsulfured molasses

Combine. It will be gloppy at first, just keep mixing until everything evens out.

To make dark brown sugar, use one part of molasses to four parts sugar (¼ c. molasses + 1 c. sugar).

Cake Flour

I don't keep cake flour on hand because I don't use a lot of it, but, as the name might give away, the lower protein content makes it great for cakes and baked goods. You do need to sift this, a lot, because the sifting ensures the ingredients are well combined and airy.

1 c. all-purpose flour, - 2 Tbsp. flour

Measure 1 c. all-purpose flour, then remove 2 Tbsp. and put it back in with the flour for use another day.

2 Tbsp. cornstarch

Add cornstarch and mix. Sift the mixture 5 times. Yes, 1, 2, 3, 4, 5 times. That's it.

Original Source: CakeWhiz.com (Homemade Cake Flour)

Cheesy Fish Crackers

What kid doesn't love these? You can try making these with other kinds of cheeses if there is no American cheese available.

> 2 slices real American cheese (not "cheese food")
> ½ tsp. salt
> ½ tsp. powdered ginger
> ⅛ tsp. garlic powder
> ⅛ tsp. chili powder

Preheat oven to 400°F. Stack American cheese slices and cut into 16 squares. You do not need to remove the plastic because *real* American cheese doesn't come in individual, plastic-encased slices. Separate the 32 squares. Combine spices, then coat the cheese squares with it. Arrange squares on a parchment paper lined baking sheet or silicone baking mat, leaving space between crackers for melting cheese. After 7-7½ minutes, they should puff up and be well-browned–almost, but not quite. They'll be soggy if they are undercooked. These are best enjoyed within a few days.

Original Source: KeyIngredient.com (Stella Style Goldfish Crackers)

Cheez Crackers

I left the dough ball in the freezer overnight and ended up with an orange rock. Don't end up with an orange rock.

> 1 c. flour
> 4 Tbsp. cold butter, cut into small pieces (*not* melted)
> 8 oz. shredded mild cheddar cheese

¾ teaspoon of sea salt

4-5 Tbsp. cold water

Combine everything but water in a food processor and pulse until mixture is crumbly. Add cold water to the cheese crumble by the tablespoon and mix it until dough forms. Roll dough into a ball and wrap it in cling wrap. Freeze dough ball for at least 30 minutes to ensure it is cold the whole way through. Colder/harder dough is easier it to handle, so don't take it out early, but don't leave it get rock solid.

Preheat oven to 350°F. Remove dough from the freezer. Put it between two sheets of parchment or wax paper. Flatten dough with a rolling pin until it's about ⅛" thick, then cut it into 1" squares with a pizza cutter or knife. Sprinkle with sea salt and bake 20-25 minutes. There is a fine line between golden and burnt, so watch carefully.

Confectioner's Sugar

I have tons of this on hand, but what I have on hand isn't the point. I also have a lot of brown sugar on hand and somehow manage to be unable to find it sometimes. In a pinch, knowing how to make your own can make life so much easier.

1 c. granulated sugar

1 Tbsp. cornstarch

Blend for a few minutes until powdery. The cornstarch is to prevent clumping. You can also use a coffee grinder.

Original Source: EugenieKitchen.com (Icing Sugar)

Graham Crackers

Again, it never occurred to me to make these at home. When I was making a graham cracker crust, I realized these were almost certainly another kind of crackers that can be made at home. So I did, but I still strongly prefer the store-bought ones.

1 c. whole wheat or graham flour

1 c. unbleached flour

¼ c. sugar

½ tsp. salt

1 tsp. cinnamon

1 tsp. baking powder

Combine in a bowl.

1 egg

¼ c. vegetable oil

¼ c. honey

2-3 Tbsp. milk

Combine in a second bowl. Mix in to dry ingredients. Dough will be fairly stiff and may be difficult for less powerful electric mixers, but it wasn't a problem mixing by hand. Add more milk, if necessary. Wrap dough in cling wrap and chill until firm, about 1 hour.

Milk for glaze

Cinnamon-sugar (optional topping)

Preheat oven to 300°F. Divide dough in half. Knead dough gently until it holds together. Roll dough out on parchment paper, 1/16" thick. Transfer from parchment paper to a baking sheet. Take second piece of dough and repeat. Brush dough with milk, then sprinkle with cinnamon-sugar, if desired. Bake 10 minutes. Remove from oven and cut crackers into rectangles with a pizza cutter but DO NOT separate them yet. Return to the oven for 18-20 minutes. Turn off the oven and leave the door open for 5 minutes. After the heat dissipates, shut the door with the crackers inside for 20 minutes.

Original Source: KingArthurFlour.com (Graham Crackers)

Granola

I skipped the coconut and used flax seed when I made this. It came out fantastic! AND we got a ton of fiber, painlessly! This is definitely a keeper.

3 c. whole rolled oats

1 pinch sea salt

1 tsp. cinnamon

½ c. maple syrup

¼ - ½ c. shaved coconut

¼ c. nuts and seeds

Butter a cookie sheet with raised sides. Preheat oven to 300°F. Combine all ingredients. Spread on pan and bake 15 minutes. Stir. Bake another 10-12 minutes. Finished granola will be slightly golden when removed from oven and crunchy after cooling. If desired, mix in cranberries, raisins, cherries, chocolate chips, etc.

Original Source: DIYNatural.com (Homemade Granola Recipe)

Marshmallows

I was amazed to see "homemade marshmallows" in a store. They smell like gym socks before adding the vanilla but end up tasty.

3 envelopes gelatin (unflavored)

½ c. cold water

Sprinkle gelatin over cold water and soak for 10 minutes.

2 c. sugar

⅔ c. corn syrup

¼ c. water

Combine sugar, corn syrup, and the remaining water in a small sauce pan and bring to a hard boil for one minute. Pour the boiling mixture into the gelatin water and mix at high speed. (This is one recipe that really does require an electric mixer.)

Warning: The mixture "climbs" the beaters, so watch them and keep pushing it down to prevent a big mess.

¼ tsp. salt

1 Tbsp. vanilla

Confectioners' sugar (for dredging)

Add salt and beat for 12 minutes. Add vanilla. Oil a piece of cling wrap and line a 9" x 9" pan with it before scraping the mixture into it. Press the mixture flat with a second piece of oiled cling wrap. Let it set for several hours before removing, then dredging with confectioners' sugar and cutting into pieces.

Matzo

The first time I made this, I added 1 c. of water at the onset. My "dough" had the consistency of cake batter! I ended up using a whole 20 oz. bag of flour and 1¼ c. of water to get the right consistency, so start with a few ounces of water and add it slowly.

> 2 c. flour (oat, rye, barley, maize, or spelt)
> ½-1 c. water

Optional Ingredients:

> 1 tsp. olive oil
> 1 tsp. honey

Preheat oven to 475°F. Line two sheets with baking parchment. Sprinkle a rolling board or clean counter with flour and put a rolling pin with it. Mix the flour, ¼ c. water, and any optional ingredients. Knead until it comes together smoothly, 3-5 minutes, slowly adding more water until dough reaches a smooth consistency. If dough is sticky, add one teaspoon of flour at a time until is smooth. If it's flaky, add water one teaspoon at a time until smooth.

Roll each egg-size piece of dough as thin as you can. Place it on a baking sheet and use a fork to prick it all over. The pricks keep it from puffing up in the oven. Matzo won't spread as it bakes so pieces can be placed close together. Bake 3-4 minutes, until crisp. As soon as one sheet goes in, start filling the next sheet so it's ready to go in when the one before it comes out.

Original Source: theKitchn.com (Try This! Homemade Matzo)

Mayonnaise

Mayonnaise is another surprise you can make at home. Homemade only lasts as few as four days, which is unsurprising since it has uncooked egg yolk. Interestingly, all the ingredients need to be room temperature when you start, including the egg. It may be tempting to skill this step and use eggs straight out of the refrigerator but when I used too-cool egg, the whole thing stayed liquid.

If you worry about eating raw egg, then pasteurize it (page 105).

> 1 room temperature egg yolk*
>
> 1 Tbsp. Dijon mustard
>
> 1 c. neutral flavored oil (grapeseed, safflower, canola)
>
> *You can place cold eggs in warm water to speed the warm-ing process, but it still takes time.

Whisk egg yolk and mustard until well mixed. Continue whisking as you add the oil in a thin stream until it is thoroughly mixed and mayo is thick enough to hang on the whisk when it's lifted.

> 1 Tbsp. vinegar**
>
> 1 tsp. lemon juice (Optional)
>
> salt and pepper to taste
>
> **Red or white wine vinegar are recommended but I found apple cider vinegar works as well.

Whisk in remaining ingredients.

Original Source: InspiredTaste.net(Homemade Mayonnaise Recipe)

Chowhound.com (Basic Mayonnaise)

Oat Flour

> Oats (plain, unflavored)*
>
> *Rolled oats are best, but instant, quick-cook, or steel work.

Put in a food processer or blender and pulse until oats are powder. Stir a few times to be sure all the oats are ground. It should take about 1 minute. You will end up with about ¾ the volume of oat flour compared to oats.

Replace all or part of wheat flour with oat or other flours. Replace 1 c. wheat flour in recipes with ¾ c. oat flour.

Panko

This is a Japanese version of breadcrumbs. The biggest differences are that the crumbs are not as fine and that neither the crust nor wheat bread are used.

> White bread, crust removed

Preheat oven to 350°F. Shred into coarse flakes; a food processor works well. Place on an edged pan, no more than ½" deep. Bake 5-10 minutes, depending on how dry (stale) the bread already is. When it is golden brown and dry, remove it from the tray. Cool and store.

Saltines

Everyone knows you can bake cookies and cakes from scratch but saltines? It never even occurred to me that saltines can be made at home until I saw this recipe.

> 2 c. flour
> 1 tsp. salt
> ⅔ c. milk
> 2 Tbsp. butter
> ½ tsp. baking soda

Preheat oven to 375°F. Combine the dry ingredients before cutting in the butter. Add milk. Form into a ball and knead briefly. Divide into pieces and roll cracker-thin on a floured board or piece of wax paper. Seriously–roll them THIN. Place on an ungreased cookie sheet. Cut into 1½ inch squares with a sharp knife or pizza cutter. Sprinkle with salt and prick with a fork to make them look like crackers. Bake at 375°F for 10 to 12 minutes or until lightly browned, taking care not to burn them.

Self-Rising Flour

"Self-rising flour" has baking powder mixed in. If you don't have any on hand, this is how you make your own.

> 1 c. all purpose flour
> 1½ tsp. baking powder

½ tsp. salt

Combine.

Shortening

Coconut oil has a lot of uses and this is generally a healthier alternative than commercially available shortening–as long as no one in the family is allergic.

¾ cup refined coconut oil

¼ cup canola, light olive oil or rice bran oil

Warm coconut oil until it is soft/barely melted. Add the oil and mix in a food processor for one minute. Scrape down container sides as necessary. It stays good for about three months in the refrigerator.

Original Source: VeganBaking.net (How to Make Vegan Shortening)

Water Crackers

1 c. flour, sifted

2 Tbsp. butter

4 Tbsp. water

Salt to taste (start with a pinch)

Preheat oven to 400°F. Mix salt and flour. Cut butter into mixture. Add water and mix well. Dough should be dry but hold together. If dough is sticky, add slightly more flour. If it's flaky, add slightly more water. Coat the dough and your rolling board lightly with flour. Roll out dough until paper thin. Thicker dough takes longer to bake and ends up less cracker-like. Cut into your preferred size and shape. Squares are easy and result in less leftovers you will need to re-roll and cut. Use a fork to poke holes in the crackers to prevent puffing up and encourage them to stay flat. Put on a cookie sheet and bake 6-8 minutes or until they start to brown.

5. Cheese and Dairy

<u>You need a good liquid thermometer for these recipes.</u>

Most of these are things most of us just buy ready-made, like evaporated milk and sour cream, but this book isn't about what we do every day. It's about how to continue enjoying a reasonably normal diet in an emergency. There is no denying these recipes require a source of fresh milk, which may not be available, but, depending on your circumstances, it might. The thing I've found really amazing is how easy these things are to make, albeit sometimes time-consuming.

There are all kinds of great cheeses you can make at home but they all seem to have one thing in common: you can't use ultra-pasteurized milk. The closer to raw it is, the better it is for cheese. Of course, raw milk is illegal some places and is hard to find almost any-where except on an actual farm. Markets like Whole Foods® and "ethnic" markets are more likely to have milk that is less pasteurized because their customers are more likely to want and need it, but our local grocer carries it too.

The brand I found is in actual glass bottles that you return so the farm can reuse them! I was confused to see "creamline" in addition to whole and 2%. Creamline milk has not been homogenized and still has cream in it, which can leave a cream line when it isn't shaken to mix it, or skim it off to use elsewhere. Creamline is less processed, so it is closer to what comes out of the cow. Some grocers may put less processed milk in a special area with farm-fresh ingredients, so it pays to ask about it at the guest services/information desk. If you enjoy the cheese recipes here, there is a whole world of cheese-making to explore.

How to Drain Whey

Quite a few dairy and cheese recipes need to have the "whey" drained and separated from the curds, just like in the nursery rhyme. When milk is curdled as part of making cheese, for example, liquid (whey) separates from the solids (curds). Whey is healthy and a quick internet search yields dozens of uses for it.

The basic process for draining whey is to line a strainer with cheese-cloth, then put the strainer over a container to catch the whey. Pour curdled milk into the cheesecloth and let whey drip into the container below. Pull the corners together and knot them to keep the contents clean and critter free. Personally, I also empty the whey periodically in case my cats decide to push it off the counter. Again. You can use a spoon or something similar to suspend the cheesecloth over the container, but I find it easier to leave it (covered) in the strainer over the container. Some, but not all, recipes have you squeeze any remaining whey out at the end. Keep the whey to use in other recipes, or feed it to a dog or chicken.

There are two basic kinds of whey. Sweet whey comes from cheeses made with rennet. Acidic whey comes from those made with vinegar, lemon juice, or something similarly acidic.

Butter/Buttermilk

You can make butter by shaking it in a jar, but it's much easier to use a machine (mixer or blender with a tight lid). It's also much easier, and faster, if you don't use ultra-high pasteurized, UHP, cream, but you can make it with that. I just wouldn't want to do it by hand.

    1 pint heavy whipping cream (or whatever you have on hand)

Start mixing cream on low and increase the speed to medium. It will first form soft, then stiff peaks. After the cream breaks, you'll either hear sloshing and then more solid chunks (if by hand) or see butter on the beaters as butterfat separates from liquids. Pour the buttermilk into a container to save for later.

> Bowl of ice water
>
> Salt to taste (optional)

Pour the ice water over the butter to rinse it. Press remaining buttermilk out with a spoon or spatula. Pour off liquid and repeat until the water runs clear. Add salt, if desired, and mix through.

Original Source: ToriAvey.com (Homemade Butter)

Buttermilk (version 2)

> 1 Tbsp. vinegar

Put vinegar in a one cup liquid measuring cup.

> Milk

Fill measuring cup up to one cup mark. Let sit for 5 minutes, then use.

Original Source: TastesofLizzyT.com (Amish Buttermilk Biscuits)

Condensed Milk (Sweetened)

You can make dairy-free condensed milk by substituting cococonut, soy, or any other kind of milk you have on hand. You can also substitute other sugars such as Stevia or Truvia.

> 2 c. full fat or low fat milk
>
> ⅔ c. sugar OR honey OR maple syrup

Combine in a saucepan over low heat. Once all the sugar dissolves, increase the temperature to medium-low and simmer. DO NOT STIR once the mix starts to simmer. If you do, it may crack and crystalize. If a skin forms, gently remove it so water can still evaporate. Simmer gently for 35-40 minutes, until milk darkens to a creamy color, reduces by half, and thickens a bit. If there is foam on top, gently skim it off with a spoon. DO NOT stir any sugary bits around the rim because it may crack the mix. Remove from heat and pour into a jar to cool but DO NOT put the airtight lid on until it has cooled completely. After a few hours in the fridge, it should thicken up quite a bit. It can last up to 6 months in the fridge.

Original Source: BiggerBolderBaking.com (How to Make Condensed Milk)

AddAPinch.com (Make Sweetened Condensed Milk)

Cottage Cheese

I have insane allergies and cottage cheese is one of my go-to foods when I'm struggling with my food issues. It's good to know I can have it even in an emergency–as long as I can get milk.

2½ c. whole or 2% milk

¼ c. vinegar

Bring milk almost to a boil, at least 185°F. Watch for bubbles to rise to the top. Immediately remove saucepan from heat. Stir in vinegar and a dash of salt (if desired). Milk should start curdling immediately. Cool completely, about 1 hour at room temperature.

Drain whey following instructions at the start of the chapter. If desired, gather the sides of the cloth around the mixture and squeeze the whey out. After it drains for about 5 minutes, you may want to rinse some of the remaining fat off the curds under a stream of cold water, moving them around to ensure they are all rinsed. Keep them in the strainer with cheesecloth while you do this. If desired, crumble the curds. Store the whey and any cottage cheese you don't eat immediately in airtight containers.

Original Source: TheOrganicPrepper.com (How to Make Cottage Cheese)

Cream Cheese

This was a lot easier than I expected, and worth knowing how to do in an emergency, especially if you make your own bagels.

2¼ c. cream (NOT ultra-heat treated, UHT)

½ c. whole milk (NOT ultra-heat treated, UHT)

2 tsp salt

¼ c. white vinegar (+ 1 Tbsp., modify to taste)

Heat cream, milk and salt over medium heat. Gently stir to decrease scorching. When it reaches 180°F; it may bubble but should not boil. Remove from heat and let set for 5 minutes. Combine gently with ¼ c. vinegar. If you want it tangier, add 1 Tbsp. of vinegar at a time until you like the taste. If you want it saltier, add ¼ tsp. of salt at a time until you like the taste. Cover loosely (this is one time airtight is bad) and leave on the counter for 8-12 hours while it cultures. A tea towel is a great "lid" for this since it allows so much air circulation. A warmer kitchen leads to faster culturing, a cold kitchen leads to slower culturing. When it generally resembles yogurt, it has set up.

Drain whey following instructions at the start of the chapter.. Dump the thickened cream into the bowl. If desired, pull up the four corners of the cheesecloth and tie them together. Suspend the ball over a bowl. Let the whey drip out for at least 12 hours. Dripping longer leads to firmer and tangier finished cheese. Scrape finished cream cheese out of the cheesecloth and lightly salt it, if desired, and refrigerate to extend the shelf life. When it feels firm and isn't dripping, it's done. It will firm up more in the refrigerator.

Original Source: MyBluprint.com (How to Make Your Own Cream Cheese)

Evaporated Milk (from fresh)

The difference between this pantry basic and Condensed Milk is that evaporated milk doesn't have added sugar.

1 liter milk (homogenized)*

*Use twice as much milk as you need evaporated milk.

Heat to simmering in a saucepan. (A thick base can reduce burning.) Whisk often to prevent a skin from forming. If a skin forms, remove or break it so water can still evaporate. Simmer until the volume reduces by about half, about 30 minutes. Milk may end up light brown or white, depending on how much it was whisked. Remove from heat. Strain milk into an airtight container.

Evaporated Milk (from dehydrated)

> 1¼ c. water
> 1 c. dehydrated milk
> 7 Tbsp. butter (optional)

Heat water to simmering. Add butter, if desired. Stir in dehydrated milk. Continue cooking until desired consistency is reached. It starts concentrated so it should only take a few minutes.

Original Source: OrganicFacts.com (How to Make Evaporated Milk)

Gjetost Cheese (pronounced "yeh-toast")

I included this Scandinavian cheese for one simple reason: all these dairy projects have left me with quite a bit of whey, and I need to use it. If you do a lot of dairy projects, you will probably have a lot of whey to use, too. If this cheese is made from cow whey instead of goat whey, it's technically mysost.

This takes *a long time* because you are boiling a gallon of liquid down to a pint of liquid. Either start it in a crock pot before bedtime, or first thing in the morning. It is important to keep it uncovered so water can evaporate out of it. If you have nosy pets, you might keep it covered just until it gets too hot for them to touch comfortably.

> 1 gallon (8 c.) whey (preferably sweet)

Bring whey to a low boil and simmer uncovered 5 hours or in a slow cooker for 12-18 hours, although I have left it on for 24 hours with no problem. Stir frequently until it reduces to about 1 pint (2 c.).

> 1 c. heavy cream

Optional Ingredients:

> 1 Tbsp. butter (to reduce foaming)

Continue simmering as you add cream and butter, stirring until you are happy with the consistency, ideally similar to thick gravy. Total

SIMPLE COOKING FOR FAMILIES

time for a slow cooker is up to 24 hours. Once it coats the back of a spoon and the liquid doesn't instantly run back when you move it, take if off the heat. Stir for several more minutes so large crystals don't form. Cool. For creamier cheese, blend. It is good warm as a pasta sauce or cold as a cracker spread. Refrigerate to store.

Original Source: JoybileeFarm.com (How to Make Gjetost from Whey)

TheHealthyHomeEconomist.com (Make Gjetost Cheese)

Goat Cheese (Chevre)

This is insanely easy to make and every bit as good as store bought cheese.

4 c. (1 qt.) goat milk

Heat the milk to 180°F over medium-low, stirring frequently to ensure even heating. Remove from heat as soon as it reaches 180°F.

⅓ c. lemon juice

2 Tbsp. vinegar

Add lemon juice and stir until just combined. Repeat with vinegar. Let sit for 30 minutes, although it can be longer. Tiny, speck-like curds will form.

½ tsp. salt

Add salt and stir lightly. Drain whey following instructions at the start of the chapter for about 1 hour using a double or triple layer of cheesecloth. Untie cheesecloth and shape cheese. Mix herbs or other mix-ins into the cheese, sprinkle them on top, or leave it plain. Refrigerate to set.

Original Source: EthnicSpoon.com (How to Make Goat Cheese Recipe)

Greek Yogurt

To make Greek-style yogurt, make yogurt and drain off the whey. It will take anywhere from 4-24 hours. If you strain it longer, you will end up with something close to cream cheese. Stir or move it after a few hours to allow the yogurt to continue to drain; if you don't you may end up with some unstrained yogurt on top. When you look at the whey, you may find some lighter yogurt under the whey, especially if you make yogurt cheese.

Half and Half

I found two recipes for this, both super simple

> 1 c. milk
> ¼ c. heavy cream

Combine 4 parts milk with 1 part heavy cream.

OR

> ¾ c. milk
> ¼ c. light whipping cream

Combine 3 parts milk with 1 part light whipping cream.

Heavy Cream

> ⅔ c. whole milk
> ⅓ c. melted butter

OR

> ⅙ c. milk
> ⅞ c. half and half

Combine ingredients.

Original Source: SimpleMost.com (Make Your Own Heavy Cream)

Mozzarella Cheese

Not surprisingly, milk is very important in cheese. Farm-fresh milk is great if you can get it. Homogenized or non-homogenized can work, but non-homogenized is better. Ultra-pasteurized will not work at all. Low fat milk will also work, but the cheese will be drier and less flavorful. SeriousEats.com has a great post "How to Make Mozzarella From Scratch" that discusses qualities to look for in milk (the less processed, the better).

If you don't use thick rubber gloves of some kind, this can get painful. The first two times I made it, I didn't knead the final cheese long enough because the hot cheese was becoming painful. Obviously, the gloves can't have been used with chemical cleaning tablets, but thick kitchen or nitrile gloves will definitely make this a more pleasant experience, and make it easier to get a good finished cheese.

$\frac{1}{4}$ rennet tablet OR $\frac{1}{4}$ tsp. single strength liquid rennet

$\frac{1}{4}$ c. cool non-chlorinated water

Crush the rennet tablet and dissolve in water, or add liquid rennet to water to help it mix into the milk more evenly. Set aside.

$1\frac{1}{2}$ tsp. citric acid

1 c. cool water

1 gallon (8 c.) milk (not ultra-pasteurized)

Combine and pour into a pot. (Not the one with the rennet.) Pour milk in quickly to help it mix properly. SLOWLY heat milk to 90°F on medium-low, 10-15 minutes. The milk may start to curdle slightly from the acidity and temperature. If the milk isn't forming a proper curd, increase the temperature to 95°F or even 100°F.

When milk reaches 90°F, remove it from the heat and slowly add rennet mixture. Stir top to bottom for 30 seconds, then return to low heat, stirring occasionally until it reaches 105°F. (Traditionally, cheese is removed from the heat, rests for 5 minutes, then cut up; stirring occasionally accomplishes the same thing and allows the cheese to be finished more quickly.) Remove from heat and let whey settle for 5-10 minutes.

Put a strainer over a bowl. Scoop curds into the strainer with a slotted spoon. Press gently on the curds to remove as much whey as possible. Put whey into an airtight container to use another time. Let curds cool for 10 minutes, then place on a cutting board. Slice into 1" cubes. (A crumbly ricotta-like texture and difficulty forming a single mass is a milk issue, try again with less pasteurized milk.)

Put curds into a bowl and microwave for 30-60 seconds, checking to ensure it doesn't overcook and turn to mush. Gently drain and squeeze more whey from the curds. Knead cheese with a spoon until it is cool enough to touch. Microwave for 35 seconds, then Drain whey following instructions at the start of the chapter. Knead. Repeat a third time.

Up to 1 tsp. kosher salt

Mix in. If it looks like ricotta and won't hold together, reheat in microwave for 20-30 seconds. Knead the curd as if it's bread dough until smooth and shiny. If it cools and becomes difficult to knead, microwave for another 30 seconds. It should become soft enough to stretch like taffy. Knead the cheese back into a smooth, shiny ball. It's ready to eat! You can let uneaten mozzarella rest in whey or room temperature water, salted to taste.

Original Source: Cheesemaking.com (30 minute mozzarella)

Ricotta Cheese

The traditional method uses the whey left over from cooking other kinds of cheese, but this one is simpler.

Scant ½ tsp. citric acid OR ¼ c. lemon juice, preferably fresh

If you use citric acid, put it in a small bowl and stir in a splash of hot-not-boiling water. Dissolve in water completely.

4 c. whole milk

Pour milk into a non-reactive pot over low heat. Use a rubber spatula to stir occasionally. When the milk starts to steam and become frothy at the edges (180°F), remove from heat and add a small amount of the citric acid mix or lemon juice. Add small amounts until the milk curdles. Let rest about 15 minutes, until pot is cool enough to touch.

¾ c. heavy cream

Line a strainer with a double or triple layer of cheesecloth and put it over a bowl. Pour in curdled milk and drain off whey. In 20-30 minutes, it should be done. Transfer curds into a bowl. Slowly and gently fold in cream until it is thick but not chunky.

Original Source: MasterClass.com (How to Make Homemade Ricotta Cheese)

Sour Cream

Depending on what kind of cream you use, sour cream thickness can vary a lot. Heavy or whipping cream is the thickest. Half-and-half is somewhat thinner, but not as thin as raw cream, if you can even find raw cream. Dehydrated milk can be added to half and half to improve the consistency. The one kind you should avoid is any cream that is ultra-pasteurized or ultra-high temperature. Whatever cream you use, homemade sour cream comes out thinner than store-bought because it doesn't have any artificial thickeners added. You can also make sour cream using sour cream starter culture.

> 1 c. heavy cream (NOT ultra-heat treated, UHT)
> 2 tsp. lemon juice OR white vinegar
> ¼ c. milk

Combine cream and lemon juice (or vinegar) in a jar. Add milk. Seal lid tightly and shake to combine all ingredients. It needs to be exposed to fresh air to be more flavorful, so remove the lid and cover it with a breathable cloth or paper towel. Secure with a rubber band and leave on a counter overnight or use a canning jar*, up to 24 hours, until it sets.

By 24 hours, it should be set. If it cultures for too long or at too high a temperature, sour cream separates. Remove the cover, stir, and re-cover with the jar lid. It should keep for about 2 weeks in the fridge.

> *A canning jar works well for this. Remove the lid after you shake it, then put it on again when you refrigerate it. The ring can hold a piece of cheesecloth firmly in place while it cultures.

Original Source: BiggerBolderBaking.com (How to Make Sour Cream)

Whipped Cream

If you mix everything in a cold metal bowl, it is even easier. This is one of the few recipes in this section that does *can* use UHP (Ultra High Pasteurized) dairy. It will work just fine, although glass-bottle cream is even better. My family was shocked by how easy it was to make and how tasty it is.

> 1½ c. heavy whipping cream (cold)
> ½ c. powdered sugar
> 1 tsp. vanilla
> OR
> 1 c. heavy whipping cream (cold)
> 1-2 Tbsp. sugar
> ½-1 tsp. vanilla

Combine. Starting on low speed and gradually increase to high, mix until stiff peaks form. Stores for up to 2 days. Re-whisk for 30 seconds, if needed.

Maple Whipped Cream

I don't know what exactly made me try this, but it was a lovely change from plain whipped cream. If you experiment, I'm sure you'll come up with even more variations on it.

> ½ Tbsp. maple syrup

Add to the whipped cream recipe above.

Original Source: SugarSpunRun.com (Homemade Whipped Cream)

Yogurt

Compared to other things in this chapter, lots of people seem to make yogurt so I didn't expect it to be the hardest thing in this book. It is actually super finicky and has to be kept in a tight temperature range. It took me three tries to get it right!

You need a starter to make yogurt, either yogurt you already have or special yogurt starter, typically a powder. I used Greek yogurt. Some brands will work better than others, ones that are fresher and have more kinds of bacteria ferment the yogurt faster. **If you use yogurt, it is very important to make sure it has live active cultures.**

4 c. milk

Optional Ingredients:

⅓ c. powdered milk

Heat the milk slowly over low-medium heat until it reaches 180°F. but do not let it boil. Add the optional powdered milk, if desired, especially for whole or 2% milk. Remove it from the heat and cool to 108-112°F, 20-30 minutes. (You can put it in the refrigerator to cool but that makes it easier to miss when it reaches the desired temperature.) If the milk isn't cool enough, it can kill the live active cultures and you won't get yogurt.

½ c. yogurt (as starter) OR equivalent yogurt starter

When milk reaches108-112°F, add a small amount to the yogurt starter to break up the yogurt and make blending easier. It also helps the yogurt cultures adjust to the higher temperature of the milk. It needs to stay between 90°F and 120°F and undisturbed while it cultures, 4-12 hours.

During this 4-12 hours, you can put it in the Wonderbag, wrap it in a towel, put it in a larger bowl full of hot water, put it in a preheated oven, or a combination. If you put it in the oven, every two hours you should turn the oven on for 5 minutes, then turn it off again. If you put it in a bowl of hot water, replace the water with new hot water every 2 hours. The yogurt will get tarter and thicker as it cultures longer. Once you are happy with the taste and texture, whisk to recombine all the ingredients. Cover and cool for 2 hours before refrigerating. Refrigerate for at least 6 hours before eating to ensure the culturing process has stopped.

Original Source: 101Cookbooks.com (Homemade Yogurt Recipe)

CulturesforHealth.com (How to Make Homemade Yogurt)

WonderbagWorld.com (Yogurt)

6. Seasonings

Cooking every single meal and snack from scratch is tough. Most of us just don't have that much time, and many of us (myself included) don't have the desire. This section has some ideas for ingredients you can make ahead in larger batches to speed up the process. You can also pre-cook and freeze meals on the weekend, and heat them up throughout the week.

When you can't just run out to the store to buy some taco mix or barbeque sauce, or you just don't want all the additives, give these a try. The barbeque and ketchup are "nightshade free", which makes them different from most recipes for those. (It means they don't have any tomatoes, among other things, which could be very handy in a real emergency if you are running short on tomatoes.) In daily life, you can freeze small portions of each condiment in ice cube trays and defrost cubes as needed, if you won't use it all immediately.

Because I am virtually unable to eat spices, I did not try most of the recipes in this section.

Butter (Flavored)

Use as you would "normal" butter. Honey butter on fresh bread is a true treat. Butter should be set out in advance so it is room temperature, softer and easier to work with, but these can be done with refrigerated butter.

Butter (Whipped)

Whip butter until light and fluffy. Gradually add ingredients, if desired. Beat a second time until you are happy with the consistency. Store until needed.

Blueberry-Honey Butter

This recipe is different from the others.

> 1 c. blueberries
> ½ c. honey
> 2 tsp. lemon juice (optional)

If desired, mash blueberries with a fork. Combine in a pan over medium to medium low heat. Bring to a low boil until the mixture turns a rich purple. Remove from heat and cool.

> 1 c. butter

Combine with butter. Follow the method for whipped butter or use a blender.

Cinnamon Butter

> 1 c. whipped butter
> ⅓ c. sweetened condensed milk
> 1 tsp. cinnamon
> 1 tsp. light corn syrup

Gradually add ingredients to whipped butter. Beat a second time until you are happy with the consistency.

Cranberry Butter

> ½ c. fresh cranberries
> 1¾ c. powdered sugar

Combine berries and sugar in a blender or food processor.

> ½ c. butter

SEASONINGS

1 Tbsp. orange juice

Add to well-combined cranberry and sugar mixture.

Honey Butter

½ c. butter

½ c. honey

½ tsp. vanilla

Use whipped butter method.

Jam Butter

½ c. butter, cubed

4 Tbsp. jam

Whip butter until light and fluffy. Gradually add ingredients. Beat a second time until you are happy with the consistency.

Maple Syrup Butter

8 oz. butter

¾ - 1 c. maple syrup

¼ - ¾ tsp. kosher salt

Set butter out in advance so it is room temperature. Whip butter until light and fluffy. Gradually add ingredients. Beat a second time until you are happy with the consistency.

Mustard Butter

4 Tbsp. butter

2 Tbsp. stone ground mustard

Whip butter until light and fluffy. Gradually add ingredients. Beat a second time until you are happy with the consistency.

Pumpkin Honey Butter

1 c. butter

¾ tsp. cinnamon

½ tsp. pumpkin pie spice

6 Tbsp. pumpkin puree (NOT pie filling)

5 Tbsp. honey

1 tsp. vanilla

Fully mix in spices and 1 Tbsp. of puree, then add the remaining puree. When that is fully mixed, add the honey and vanilla.

Strawberry Vanilla Butter

8 Tbsp. butter

1 pack (.33 oz) dehydrated strawberries

1 Tbsp.vanilla

Whip butter until light and fluffy. Gradually add ingredients. Beat a second time until you are happy with the consistency.

Sundried Tomato Butter

8 Tbsp. butter

Whip butter until light and fluffy.

1 Tbsp. sundried tomatoes

Chop tomatoes into paste in a food processor. Gradually add to butter. Beat a second time until you are happy with the consistency.

Original Source: SomewhatSimple.com (Blueberry Honey Butter)

SavorySimple.net (Whipped Maple Butter)

LittleDairyOnthePrairie.com (Whipped Cinnamon Butter)

Brit.co (30 Homemade Butter Recipes)

Caribbean Jerk Dry Rub

This is for burgers.

1 Tbsp. onion flakes

1 Tbsp. garlic powder

2 tsp. ground thyme

2 tsp. sugar

2 tsp. dried chives

2 tsp. kosher salt

1 tsp. allspice

¾ tsp. pepper

½ tsp. cayenne

½ tsp. nutmeg

¼ tsp. cinnamon

Combine ingredients. To use, sprinkle both sides of burgers or other meat. Rub it in.

Original Source: TheGardeningCook.com (Caribbean Jerk Dry Rub)

Italian Seasoning

This is readily available at grocery stores, but it's always nice to be able to personalize it to your families' taste, and to use garden-fresh spices.

3 Tbsp. dried parsley

3 Tbsp. dried basil

2 Tbsp. oregano

1 Tbsp. garlic powder

1 tsp. rosemary

1 tsp. thyme

1 tsp. onion powder

½ tsp. red pepper flakes

¼ tsp. pepper

Combine ingredients.

Original Source: ACultivatedNest.com (Homemade Italian Seasoning)

Old Bay® Seasoning

This is a mid-Atlantic classic, particularly anywhere with Blue Crabs. If Maryland had an official state spice, it would definitely be Old Bay. If you live anywhere with crabs and don't already know Old Bay, this is one recipe you should definitely try. (Since "the real deal" is a blend of 18 herbs and spices, this won't be exactly the same.)

1 Tbsp. celery salt

3 tsp. ground bay leaves

1½ tsp. yellow mustard powder

1 tsp. pepper

1 tsp. smoked paprika

¾ tsp. nutmeg

½ tsp. sweet paprika

½ tsp. white pepper

¼ tsp. all spice

¼ tsp. cardamom

1 pinch ground cloves

1 pinch ground ginger

Combine ingredients. Store in an airtight container.

Original Source: SprinklesAndSprouts.com (Homemade Old Bay Seasoning)

Poultry Seasoning

4 tsp. dried sage

3 tsp. dried thyme

2 tsp. dried marjoram

1 tsp. dried rosemary

¼ tsp. pepper

⅛ tsp. nutmeg

Combine ingredients Blend until well mixed. Store in an airtight container until ready to use. You can also use fresh herbs.

Original Source: SimpleVeganBlog.com (Poultry Seasoning)

Ramen Seasoning

2 Tbsp. poultry seasoning

2 Tbsp. garlic powder

2 Tbsp. onion powder

2 chicken-flavored bouillon cubes

1 tsp. pepper (more to taste)

SEASONINGS

Crush bouillon cubes into a powder in a food processor, with a mortar and pestle, or by hand. Combine ingredients. Store in an airtight container until ready to use.

Original Source: FunHappyHome.com (Homemade Ramen Seasoning)

Salt (Flavored)

Chefs add flavored salt to food at the very end, as a finishing flourish, but it can also be used as a marinade base, in place of regular salt, or for a meat or vegetable rub. Flavored salt adds big flavor with a small amount of an ingredient. After trying a recipe or two, get creative and make your own, or search online for more recipes. I added maple syrup on a whim and it's quite tasty with breakfast recipes.

Basic Flavored Salt

Combine ingredients in a clean coffee grinder or small food processor. (If you use a coffee grinder, make sure the primary coffee drinker knows and approves.) Use coarse salt, such as sea salt or kosher salt. Pulse until all ingredients are uniformly small. Store the herbed salt in a glass jar, such as an empty vitamin jar. Put a small amount of rice in the bottom if moisture is a concern. Change the amounts of herbs and flavorings to suit your own taste.

If you use a liquid such as vanilla, maple syrup, or lemon juice, sprinkle over salt before grinding to ensure even distribution, rather than pouring it all into one spot. If you use herbs, they should be dry but not brown. Salt with fresh herbs or moist ingredients like garlic can be dried by baking it in the oven for 1-2 hours at 170-180°F and may need to be ground a second time after being removed from the oven to break up clumps.

Garlic Salt

½ c. salt
2 cloves garlic

Garlic can be roasted or not. Crush cloves and chop with salt.

Herbed Salt

½ c. salt

10 sprigs of dried herbs such as rosemary, oregano, or lemon balm

Destem and coarsely chop herbs.

Lavender Salt

½ c. salt

3 tsp. dried lavender

Maple Syrup Salt

½ c. salt

2 tsp. maple syrup

Mushroom Salt

½ c. salt

½ oz. dried shitake mushrooms

Rosemary and Lemon Salt

½ c. salt

3 tsp. dried lemon zest

3 tsp. dried rosemary

If you make fresh lemon zest, use a microplane zester to remove the outer zest and only the outer part, not the inner part, which is bitter. Allow to dry on a towel for a few hours before combining with other ingredients. Destem and coarsely chop rosemary.

Original Source: MommyPotamus.com (flavored salt)

Shake and Bake

This is a classic people tend to forget about but it's also a good way to use stale bread, by turning it into bread crumbs.

3 c. bread crumbs

¼ c. vegetable oil

1 Tbsp. salt

1 Tbsp. dried onion flakes

3 tsp. paprika

1 tsp. garlic powder

1 tsp. black pepper

½ tsp. cayenne pepper

½ tsp. dry parsley

½ tsp. dry basil

½ tsp. dry oregano

Combine all ingredients. Mix until bread crumbs and oil are no longer clumpy. Store at room temperature. To use, dump some of mix into a gallon zippered plastic bag. Rinse chicken or other protein. When excess water is gone, put it in the bag, seal it, then shake to coat. Remove and put on a lined cookie sheet. Bake at 425°F for 15-20 minutes.

Original Source: TheBlackPeppercorn.com (Homemade Shake n Bake)

Sloppy Joe Seasoning

1 Tbsp. minced onion

1 tsp. salt

1 tsp. corn or potato starch

1 tsp. minced garlic

¼ tsp. mustard powder

¼ tsp. celery seed

¼ tsp. chili powder

Combine ingredients. Store in an airtight container until ready to use.

Original Source: LittleHouseLiving.com (Sloppy Joe Seasoning Mix)

Taco Seasoning

Optional Ingredients (add as your health allows):

1 Tbsp. chili powder

2 tsp. cumin

½ tp. garlic powder

1 tsp. paprika

¼ tsp. oregano

½ tsp. onion powder

1 tsp. salt

¼ tsp. crushed red pepper

½ tsp. pepper

Combine ingredients. Store in an airtight container until ready to use.

Original Source: TastyThin.com (Homemade Taco Seasoning Mix)

Tomato (and Onion and Garlic) Powder

If you have a bumper crop of tomatoes, onions, or garlic, this is a great way to save some of them for later.

seeded tomatoes, onions, or garlic

Seed your tomato slices before dehydration. Once you have crispy tomato slices, break them into small pieces and turn them into powder using your food processor or blender.

Follow the same process for onion or garlic powder.

When I used my food processor to make tomato powder, enough powder worked its way between the lid and the body of the main container that it got stuck. I dumped it upside down and shook all the powder out through the opening where it came in, then had to rinse it with water until it finally opened, so be careful to open the container fairly often to keep from having that happen to you.

7. Dips, Sauces, and Condiments (including dessert)

Sauces, dips, and toppings are a good way to add variety to your meals and to use ingredients that might be starting to go bad. I find it very discouraging to eat bland meal after bland meal. Just like with condiments, you can freeze small portions of each sauce in ice cube trays and defrost cubes as needed, if you won't use the entire batch immediately. Sauces make it easy to mix and match and find something you enjoy. I made chicken breasts, cut them into pieces, and added them to the White Sauce and couscous. You get the idea—mix and match for variety and to get meals you enjoy.

If you really want to get better at sauces, there is something called the "5 mother sauces." Mastering these allows cooks to make all kinds of variations. If you want to learn more about them, a quick online search should yield a ton of information.

General Instructions for Mustard

Because of mustard's versatility, I included multiple recipes. The basic process is to combine mustard and vinegar, season in a non-reactive bowl, and let set at room temperature for 2-3 days. Refrigerate the finished mustard. Pretty simple, really.

SIMPLE COOKING FOR FAMILIES

- There are different kinds of mustard seeds. Darker ones give a stronger flavor.
- Reactive cookware (aluminum, copper, cast iron) may impart a metallic taste to mustard. Stainless steel, enamel, and glass are safer choices.
- Don't let mustard seeds/powder set too long before using or the mustard may taste harsh.
- Mustard powder can be used instead of mustard seeds Horseradish and honey are popular additions to mustard, and both are low histamine.
- but both need liquid added before you start the recipe. If you use seeds, soften in liquid for 1-2 days before starting. With powder, add liquid and let set overnight.
- Water and beer are both popular liquids to use, but it's a matter of personal taste.
- Mustard should keep for up to 2 weeks (in containers and refrigerated) but may need a bit of water whisked in if it gets too thick.

Apple Dip

    8 oz. cream cheese
    ½ c. brown sugar
    1 Tbsp. vanilla

Combine. Add extra brown sugar if it's too thin, vanilla if it's too thick.

Banana Sauce

If you don't want to make banana bread, this is another great option for almost-expired bananas.

    Almost-expired bananas
    2 Tbsp. butter
    ½ c. rum
    2-3 Tbsp. brown sugar (to taste)

Mash bananas. Simmer with butter and rum until soft. Sweeten with brown sugar. If desired, add cinnamon or nutmeg to taste.

Original Source: Van

Barbeque Sauce

This is nothing like a regular barbeque sauce but in an emergency, you may need to be able to make things without using "the usual" ingredients, which this does. It uses root vegetables, which store better for longer.

    1 Tbsp. goat's butter or vegetable oil

    1 onion

    1 garlic clove

    6 large carrots (about 4 c.)

Roughly chop onions, garlic, and carrots. Sauté in butter or oil.

    1 medium beetroot roughly chopped (about ⅔ c.)

    5 c. water

Roughly chop the beetroot. Add beets and water and simmer covered for at least 40-50 minutes, until everything is thoroughly cooked.

    ⅓ c. balsamic vinegar

    4 Tbsp. white vinegar

    2 Tbsp. fish sauce

    1 Tbsp. Dijon mustard

    ⅓ c. honey

    1 tsp. salt

    Dash of pepper

Add remaining ingredients. Puree.

Original Source: NoTomato.wordpress.com (Nightshade Free BBQ Sauce)

Berry Compote

This actually has a ton of uses, even more than jam. I particularly like it as a cheesecake topping and pie filling. It's also good in yogurt. This is a strong candidate for canning.

　　1 Tbsp. butter
　　2 Tbsp. honey
　　2 c. (1 pint) mixed berries
　　2 tsp. fresh lemon juice

Melt butter over medium heat in a saucepan. Add remaining ingredients and bring to a boil. Reduce heat and simmer, covered, for 5 minutes. Berry compote can be used on cheesecake, in pie, with yogurt, or on waffles or pancakes in place of syrup.

Brown Sugar Glaze

A classic for ham, this can be used for other meats, too. Meat should be mostly (not entirely) cooked before applying the glaze.

　　½ c. pineapple (or orange) juice
　　½ c. brown sugar
　　¼ tsp. ground ginger
　　2 tsp. cornstarch
　　2 Tbsp. Dijon mustard

Combine ingredients. Bring to a boil, then reduce heat and simmer 2-3 minutes. Cool. Brush glaze onto meat and finish cooking. Glaze should be caramelized and meat should be heated to a safe temperature (temp varies based on what the meat is).

Original Source: SpendWithPennies.com (Baked Ham with Brown Sugar Glaze)

Caramel

This is harder to make than the microwave version, but microwaves may be unavailable in an emergency. Caramel is French. The slightly thinner (and easier to make) Dulce de Leche is Spanish, but they are similar and there are recipes for both in this book.

1½ sticks butter

½ c. sugar

3 Tbsp. light corn syrup

14 oz. (1 can) sweetened condensed milk

Combine butter and sugar in a sauce pan over medium heat. Stir until melted, then add corn syrup and condensed milk. Bring to a rapid boil, decrease heat to medium and simmer, stirring constantly to avoid burning, for 7-10 minutes or until it is a deep gold and begins to pull away from pan edges.

½ tsp. vanilla

Sea salt*

*This would be a good use of flavored salt from Chapter 4.

Add vanilla. Line an 8x8 pan with waxed paper or foil and pour caramel into it. Sprinkle sea salt on top, if desired. Allow to cool completely, up to two hours. Cut into squares and wrap in wax paper.

Original Source: LeCremeDeLaCrumb.com (Easy 4 Ingredient Soft Caramels)

Caramel (microwave)

The first caramel recipe is a traditional stove-top version but I love how fast and easy this is. In addition to individual caramels, you can use this to top shortbread, on ice cream, in other candies, or simply dipped in chocolate.

¼ c. butter

½ c. white sugar

½ c. brown sugar

½ c. light corn syrup

½ c. sweetened condensed milk

½ tsp. vanilla

Combine all ingredients. Microwave 6 minutes, stirring every 2 minutes and after its done Add vanilla. Line a pan no larger than 8x8 pan with parchment paper, waxed paper, or greased foil and pour caramel into it. (Trust me, you do NOT want to put it on ungreased aluminum foil!)

Optional Ingredients:

  Sea salt

Sprinkle sea salt on top, if desired. Allow to cool completely, up to two hours. Cut into squares and wrap in wax paper. An 8x8 pan will yield very thin caramels unless you double or triple the batch.

Original Source: Kat's Kreations FaceBook (Six-Minute Caramels – MICRO-WAVE!)

Chinese Mustard

I was blown away when I saw how simple this recipe is. It uses Chinese mustard powder, which is definitely spicier.

  ¼ c. Chinese mustard powder
  ¼ c. cold water

Combine and let sit for one hour. Remember to use a non-reactive bowl. (That is the entire recipe. I wasn't joking when I said it was simple.) If it's too spicy, you can add ⅛ tsp. of cooking oil.

Chocolate Sauce

When I saw this recipe, I knew I had to include it because of the absolute flexibility to use whatever you have on hand.

  Chocolate (white, dark, milk–any kind)
  Milk, half and half, heavy cream, other liquid that combines well

Optional Ingredients:

  Pats of Butter (or sugar), esp. with very dark chocolate
  Salt, vanilla, mint, chili, etc. for flavor

Start heating water in a wide skillet. It needs to be barely simmering when you add the bowl with chocolate. Chop chocolate medium fine. Weigh it if you don't already know the weight. (1 c. medium fine chopped chocolate is about 6 oz.) Combine 1 Tbsp. liquid per ounce of chocolate in a stainless steel bowl. Put the bowl in the skillet of simmering water. Stir often until the chocolate is melted.

If you use high percentage chocolate (generally darker or more bitter chocolates), sauce may look curdled or overly thick. Slowly stir in more liquid until sauce is smooth with the desired consistency. If the chocolate flavor is too intense, slowly stir in a pat of butter or a teaspoon of sugar at a time until you like the flavor

Original Source: Food52.com (Spur-of-the-Moment Dark Chocolate Sauce)

Cinnamon Glaze

This is great for donuts and pastries.

> 1 c. confectioners' sugar
> 3-4 Tbsp. milk
> 1 tsp. cinnamon

Mix until well combined. Drizzle over donuts or other pastry.

Cinnamon Topping

> 2 Tbsp. brown sugar
> ½ c. plain yogurt
> 1 Tbsp. sour cream
> ⅛ tsp. vanilla
> Dash cinnamon

Combine well. Serve with fruit like peaches, bananas, or berries.

Dulce de leche

This is similar to caramel. Caramel is French, based on "burnt" sugar, and dates to the mid-17th century. Dulce de leche is a more modern (and thinner) Spanish dessert based on condensed milk. This recipe is written for the Wonderbag, so you use a pot without a handle, like Corningware®, and a tight-fitting lid to reduce spilling. You should be able to put a trivet under the cans and 1" of water on top of them. Dulce de leche can also be made from whey.

1 or more cans condensed milk

Remove labels from the cans. Choose a saucepan that fits all the cans laying on their sides with a trivet underneath and 1" water over top. Put the trivet in with the cans in on their sides on top of it. Cover with water so cans are submerged under at least 1" of water. Bring to a boil for 25 minutes. Cover with a tight-fitting lid. Put lidded pot in the Wonderbag for 8-12 hours.

OR simmer for 2-3½ hours on the stovetop. The longer you cook it, the darker and thicker the end result. Remove cans and allow to cool to room temperature before opening and stirring. Transfer anything you won't use immediately to jars or storage containers and refrigerate. Will keep in the refrigerator for up to a month.

Original Source: WonderBagWorld.com (Dulce de Lece (Condensed Milk))

Egg Wash

If you bake a lot, it may seem silly to include something this basic but an egg wash is a simple way to customize baked goods, in particular. An egg wash is just an egg diluted with a liquid, most commonly water, and brushed on food to give it a shiny, beautiful finish or to help toppings adhere. Pie is a perfect example. Not only does an egg wash give it a beautiful, shiny finish, if you use it between the top and bottom crust, it can have an even better seal

> 1 egg white or whole egg
> 2 Tbsp. water
> Pinch salt

Beat the egg white. Add remaining ingredients. Brush on top.

Gravy

> 3 Tbsp. cornstarch
> 2 Tbsp. water

In a small bowl, dissolve cornstarch in water. Set aside.

> 6 Tbsp. butter
> ¼ c. flour

Melt butter. Add flour. Cook 5 minutes, stirring regularly, until it turns golden brown.

20 oz. beef broth

10 oz. chicken broth

Pepper to taste

Add broth. Whisk. To thicken, add small amounts of cornstarch mix for about half, total. Add pepper to taste. Serve warm.

Hard Sauce

This is from a cookbook my Grandma gave me, which is kind of funny because I don't ever recall seeing her drink.

½ c. butter

2 c. confectioners' sugar

2 Tbsp. bourbon, brandy, sherry, or other flavorful liquor

Cream butter. Gradually add sugar. When thoroughly creamed together, add liquor and beat until light. This is lovely drizzled over angel food cake.

Herbed Dipping Sauce

½ c. mayonnaise

2 Tbsp. fresh herbs (basil, parsley, oregano, dill, etc.)

1 tsp. salt

½ tsp. pepper

Combine until smooth. Refrigerate.

Original Source: *Air Fryer Cookbook* (Crispy Fries with Herbed Dipping Sauce)

Honey Mustard

I love honey mustard. It's my favorite on sandwiches and chicken nuggets alike. I even use it on fries instead of ketchup!

¼ c. honey

¼ c. dijon mustard

1 Tbsp. yellow mustard

¼ c. mayonnaise

¼ tsp. cayenne

¼ tsp. garlic powder

Whisk everything together. It can be served immediately but flavors will combine better if it chills for two hours first. Store in refrigerator.

Original Source: CookiesandCups.com (Easy Honey Mustard)

Hot Fudge

This is a classic topping for ice cream, Twinkies®, and all kinds of desserts. Plus, it's great for dipping fruit in! Sadly, it freezes fast and gets super sticky on ice cream, so chocolate sauce might be a better choice for ice cream.

1 c. sugar

1 Tbsp. light corn syrup

1-3 Tbsp. cocoa powder

½ -¾ c. milk (should be 'soupy')

Bring to heavy boil for at least 5 minutes.

¼ - ¾ tsp. vanilla

Add vanilla and stir vigorously. Cool.

Original Source: Denise, Sister of Bob

Ketchup

This has a very mild taste, especially without the onions I am allergic to, but the color and texture mimic regular ketchup surprisingly well. It sounds weird and definitely takes some time to cook, but this nightshade-free recipe relies on ingredients that are easily stored long-term. Instead of vine-ripened tomatoes, it uses root vegetables including carrots, beets, and onions, which have long shelf-lives.

1 c. carrots

⅔ c. red beet

½ c. yellow onion

Peel and dice carrots, beets, and onions. Add to boiling water. Boil on medium-high for 15 minutes, until thoroughly cooked. Strain.

> ⅔ c. water
>
> ½ c. apple cider vinegar with the mother
>
> ½ c. honey
>
> 1 tsp. sea salt
>
> ⅛ tsp. clove
>
> ⅛ tsp. allspice (or double the clove)

Add remaining ingredients and blend until liquefied. Return to the stovetop. After mixture returns to a boil, reduce to low heat and simmer 30 minutes. It cooks down and thickens to the consistency of ketchup.

Original Source: HeWontKnowItsPaleo.com (No-Nightshade Ketchup)

Plum Sauce

This plum sauce (tkelemi) from the Republic of Georgia (the Asian country not the American state) was recommended as a possible substitute for ketchup as well as a sauce for meat and fish. I made one successful batch of plum sauce with nothing more than plums and a bit of salt when my allergies were acting up. I'm sure similar sauces could be made with other fruits.

> 1½ lb. plums*
>
> *Traditional versions of plum sauce use un-ripened (green) or slightly under-ripened sour plums (tkemali) but Santa Rosas work too. They don't use anything too sweet.

Put plums in a saucepan with water. Bring to a boil and simmer until soft, 10-15 minutes. While they are boiling, start on the spices (below). After simmering, cut plums in half. Remove pits and skin. Put soft plums through a sieve or food mill and return to a clean pan over medium heat. Bring to a boil, stirring for 3 minutes.

> 1 Tbsp. fresh mint
>
> ⅓ c. cilantro or dill

Finely mince cilantro/dill and mint.

> 2 large garlic cloves
> ¾ tsp. whole coriander
> 1 tsp. fennel seed
> 1 tsp. cayenne or chili pepper
> ½ tsp. salt

Peel and roughly chop the garlic. Pound the coriander seed, fennel seed, garlic, cayenne, and salt in a mortar and pestle to create a fine paste.

After returning plums to a boil, add spice paste and cook until the mixture thickens slightly, about 5 minutes. Stir in minced mint and cilantro. If it foams, you can skim off the foam. Remove from heat. While still hot, pour into a jar, if desired, then seal the jar for longer storage. Cool to room temperature to use and store in the refrigerator for near-term use. 1½ lbs. of plums cooks down to about 8 oz.

Original Source: PaleoFood.com (Plum Sauce (Tkemali))

LegenRecipes.com (Sauce tkemali)

Raspberry Vinaigrette

This is amazing on cranberry salad, among other things.

> ½ c. raspberries
> ¼ c. red wine vinegar
> 2-3 Tbsp. honey
> ½ tsp. salt
> ¼ tsp. pepper
> ½ c. olive oil

Optional Ingredients:

> ¼ c. fresh basil

Combine all ingredients except olive oil in a food processor or blender. Keep the processor/blender running and slowly add the oil until everything emulsifies. Set at room temperature for a few minute before serving. Stores for 3-4 days in the refrigerator but you'll need to whisk before serving.

Original Source: MommysHomeCooking.com (Raspberry Vinaigrette)

Roasted Red Pepper Sauce

When I finished this sauce, I was surprised to realize it can be used in recipes that normally use tomato sauce, like pasta. It's really quite a versatile sauce.

> 4 red bell peppers
> ¼ tsp. pepper
> ½ tsp. olive oil

Preheat the oven to 350°F. Slice peppers along the spines. Discard the seeds, stems, and white spines. Put them on a cookie sheet and bake for 25-30 minutes, until the skins start to separate. The skin will start to brown and become wrinkled. Remove skins and puree all ingredients together.

Salsa

> 28 oz. whole plum tomatoes, incl. juice
> 1 small white onion
> 1-2 jalapeno peppers
> 3 cloves garlic
> 1½ tsp. cumin (to taste)
> 1 tsp. salt
> ¼ - 1 tsp. sugar
> 1-2 handfuls cilantro
> 3 Tbsp. lime juice (approximately)

Peel and roughly chop onions. Seed and chop jalapenos. Chop garlic.

In the order listed, put all ingredients into a food processor. Pulse to break up larger pieces and process until it's the desired chunkiness. Flavor is best if it sets for a few hours to a day before eating.

Original Source: TheChunkyChef.com (5 Minute Restaurant Salsa)

Tartar Sauce

I love tartar sauce but I can't have many spices. I am ridiculously happy to have found such a simple recipe for it! The funny thing about this recipe is that it's from an air fryer cookbook but it isn't actually cooked at all!

¼ c. mayonnaise

2 Tbsp. sweet pickle relish

1 tsp. lemon juice

Combine. Refrigerate. It's that easy.

Original Source: *Air Fryer Cookbook* (Easy Tartar Sauce)

Teriyaki Sauce

My kids love teriyaki sauce. When I sought out a a good recipe years ago, all the recipes I found included sake, which I didn't want. Lo and behold, I have found the simple recipe I sought!

¼ - ½ c. soy sauce

¼ - ½ c. water

1 Tbsp. cornstarch

You need a total of ¾ cup of soy sauce and water. More soy sauce makes it more flavorful, but more water conserves soy sauce if you are running short. Whisk together until smooth.

Optional Ingredients:

2-4 Tbsp. rice vinegar (to taste)

4 Tbsp. crushed pineapple

2 Tbsp. pineapple juice

1 clove garlic (minced)

1 tsp. grated ginger

Add remaining desired ingredients. Heat over medium-high until warm.

4-5 Tbsp. honey (to taste)

Whisk in honey so it dissolves. Boil. Reduce to medium, whisking constantly. It both thickens and burns quickly, so don't walk away. Slowly add additional water if it gets too thick. It is finished when desired thickness is reached. It will thicken more as it stands. Whisk in a few Tbsp. of warm water to thin it, if needed.

Original Source: TheAdventureBite.com (3 Ingredient Easy Teriyaki Sauce)

White Sauce (Pizza or Pasta)

This makes enough for a plate of noodles or one pizza.

2 Tbsp. butter

3 Tbsp. flour

1 c. milk

¼ tsp. salt

⅛ tsp. pepper

½ c. grated cheese (parmesan, Havarti, other)

1 garlic clove, minced

2 tsp. Italian seasoning

Melt butter in a saucepan over medium heat. Slowly whisk in the milk, then the flour. Mix in remaining ingredients. Turn off heat once cheese has melted. Sauce will thicken as it stands.

Original Source: CompletelyPizza.com (White Pizza Sauce)

8. Drinks

Since drinks take a lot of storage space and we really only *need* water, most people only store water. But only drinking water can get boring pretty quickly. These drinks are all based around easily stored dry ingredients, to provide some variety in an emergency. A few drinks use milk, but dry milk is widely available and the spices will help it taste better.

Since the need for coffee or tea doesn't go away just because electricity has, there are recipes for cold brew coffee, several kinds of tea, and a chai mix that you just add to water. It may seem silly to include things as simple as coffee and iced tea, but many of us just buy them today, plus kids often have no clue how to make them. And of course, some people might find a new favorite in here. My favorite drink in this chapter is actually the roasted orange juice, but it takes a lot of time to make much.

Rehydration solution is also included because everyone gets sick and if you don't have Pedialyte™, that can be a real problem.

A Note on Iced Tea

There are lots of kinds of tea, whole books are written on it. Most of the recipes included here are for iced tea. While working on those, I learned of "family size" tea bags. They are designed primarily for iced tea and are equal to 3-4 standard size bags, or approximately 7 oz. There are even gallon size bags, equal to 4 family size bags or 16 regular bags! Quite a few companies, including Southern favorites Lipton® and Luzianne® have blends specially made for cold brew, iced tea, and sweet tea. Lipton and Luzianne also have tea recipes on their websites including a tea-time ice cream float and hot holiday spiced tea.

Arnold Palmer

This is pretty simple and my youngest loves it. There are recipes for the component drinks here, so I figured would include this.

> Lemonade
> Iced or Sweet Tea

Combine equal amounts. Refrigerate. Drink.

Chai Mix

Chai tea is very common in India. This milk-based tea tastes far milder than many "regular" black teas but the cinnamon and spices keep it from being bland. This dry mix makes quite a few cups of tea quickly and easily with no need to stand over the stove. For a fresh version, see the next recipe.

> ¼ c. nonfat dry milk powder
> ¼ c. powdered non-dairy creamer
> ¼ c. French vanilla flavored powdered non-dairy creamer
> ½ tsp. ground ginger
> ½ tsp. ground cinnamon
> ¼ tsp. ground cloves
> ¼ tsp. ground cardamom
> 6 Tbsp. unsweetened instant tea*
> *You can skip this and use tea bags with the mix when you drink it.

Combine. In a blender or food processor, blend 1 c. at a time, until mixture is the consistency of fine powder. You can also mix all ingredients except the tea. In this case, add a teabag or a strainer/tea ball with loose-leaf tea to the boiling water.

To serve, add 2 Tbsp. to 1 c. boiling water. If it tastes watery, add extra mix.

Chai Tea

I love chai tea. If you want an easily carried or longer-lasting version, try the chai mix in the previous recipe.

> 1 c. milk
> one pinch ground ginger
> one pinch ground cardamom
> one pinch ground cinnamon
> one pinch ground cloves
> 1 tsp. or 1 bag black tea

Heat milk until bubbles start to form. Be careful not to scald or burn it. Adds spices and tea. Simmer five minutes, then drink.

> 1c. fresh milk = 1 c. water + 3 Tbsp. powdered milk

Chia Seed Water

Soaked chia seeds can help retain electrolytes and hydration. They are also a good source of fiber. Seeds absorb water and have a gel-like texture.

> 1 tsp. chia seeds
> 1 glass water

Combine. Let stand 10 minutes.

Coffee (cold brewed)

When you finish a batch of cold brew coffee, you essentially have a coffee concentrate. Since you add water to taste when you heat it up, this lasts longer than a similarly-sized "regular" pot. You end up with a less bitter beverage than using hot-water brewing.

> coffee beans

water

Put ground coffee beans in a pot with cold water and cover with cling wrap or a lid. Let it set at room temperature for 12 (yes, twelve) hours to 24 hours to finish brewing. Pour the resulting coffee though a coffee filter or piece of cheesecloth to remove the grounds. Strain two or even three times to remove more grounds. Put your coffee in the fridge and heat it when you are ready to drink.

Eggnog

Eggnog traditionally uses raw eggs, which clearly is a salmonella risk. This risk can be made negligible simply by pasteurizing the eggs (page 109). Of course, many traditional versions also use alcohol, which this does not.

> 4 eggs, pasteurized

Whip until frothy on top and lemony colored, 1-2 minutes.

> ⅓ c. sugar (to taste)
> ⅛ tsp. nutmeg
> 2 Tbsp. lemon juice
> ⅛ tsp. salt

Whisk in spices.

> 4 c. milk
> ½ c. heavy cream

Add dairy and beat another 1-2 minutes. Finished eggnog will be frothy. Enjoy!

For cooked eggnog, heat the milk and cream over medium heat to 115-120°F. Slowly pour ¾ c. into whipped eggs, continuing to whip constantly to temper the eggs. Pour the entire tempered egg mixture into the milk, whisking continually. Do not use the lemon juice for cooked eggnog! Add the remaining ingredients to milk/egg mixture and continue heating over medium-low until it is 160°F, remembering to whisk constantly. If it becomes too thick, simply add some milk.

Original Source: TastesOfLizzyT.com (Homemade Eggnog)

Ginger Tea

    1" piece of ginger

    1 c. water

    Honey to taste

Peel ginger and cut into thin slices. Boil water. Add ginger and simmer 15 minutes. Strain to remove ginger. Add honey to taste.

Golden Milk

    2 c. milk

    1 tsp. dried turmeric*

    1 tsp. dried ginger*

    honey to taste

    *½" fresh thinly sliced or diced fresh turmeric or ginger can replace dried.

Heat milk in saucepan over medium heat. Stir in spices. Small bubbles will form on saucepan sides when milk starts simmering. Stir. Continue to stir and heat one-two more minutes. Do not let milk overheat! Turn off heat, cover, and let mixture set for ten minutes for better infusion. Strain if you used fresh ingredients and serve warm.

Hot Cocoa

Hot cocoa is a wonderful treat when it's cold outside. Our youngest particularly enjoys it with whipped cream and shaved chocolate curls. Our eldest simply adds marshmallows. I prefer to add a few drops of cherry, or peppermint, or orange, extract, although the allergy risks of that should be clear. Chocolate isn't compliant, but it sure is tasty, and hot cocoa somehow manages to make a nice, fresh snowfall even more magical.

    1 c. cocoa powder

    1-2 c. confectioners' (powdered) sugar*

    2½ c. powdered milk

*Powdered sugar is finer than granulated sugar, making it better for cocoa.

Combine and store in a sealed container. To make a cup, combine ⅓ to ½ c. mix and 1 c. hot water. Mix well, then add flavoring, marshmallows, or whipped topping. For chocolate curls, use a vegetable peeler to shave chocolate from a plain chocolate bar (no nuts, etc. added in).

The original recipe called for 2 c. powdered sugar, which seemed excessive to me. I tried it without any powdered sugar but that was far too bitter. One cup of powdered sugar made it enjoyable, but not sweet, especially with a few drops of cherry extract.

Optional mix-ins and toppings:

flavor extracts: ½ tsp. of vanilla, cherry, mint, orange, etc.

spices: ⅛ tsp. cinnamon, ⅛ tsp. nutmeg, 1 cinnamon stick

chocolate chips, sprinkles, curls

homemade marshmallows

mint: ½ tsp. mint extract, 3 Tbsp. crushed peppermint candy or peppermint sticks, OR 2-3 Tbsp. crème de menthe

citrus: ½ tsp orange extract OR 2-3 Tbsp. orange liqueur

Swiss mocha: 2-2½ tsp. powdered instant coffee

Canadian: ½ tsp. maple extract

Iced Tea (cold brewed)

There are almost infinite varieties of tea and additives to make iced tea exactly what suits your taste. This is for 1 qt.

4 c. cold water (cold – not just cool)

3 Tbsp. loose tea OR 5 tea bags.

Combine in a pitcher. Refrigerate, covered, 15-36 hours, until desired strength. Strain loose tea, if it isn't in a tea ball, or remove tea bags.

Iced Tea (hot brewed)

Ginger, vanilla, cucumber, cinnamon, lavender, berries…. There are tons of ways to give iced tea some variety. This makes 2 qts.

8 c. water

3 Tbsp. loose tea OR 6 tea bags.

Bring water to a simmer then remove from heat. Add tea and steep 4 minutes, until it's as strong as you like. If the loose tea isn't in a tea ball, then strain it out with a fine-mesh sieve. Cool and pour into a pitcher. Cover and refrigerate.

Peanut Butter Grape Smoothie

I'll admit it: this didn't sound even remotely appetizing, but I really wanted a different option for a smoothie recipe. This could definitely be made with room-temperature grapes (maybe even jelly) and is a good way to use up yogurt before it goes bad if you lose power.

1 Tbsp. peanut butter OR 2 Tbsp. peanut powder

1½ c. frozen seedless grapes

½ c. Greek yogurt

½ c. milk (whatever kind you can tolerate)

Combine in a blender. Blend. Drink.

Original Source: Epicurious.com (Peanut Butter and Grape Smoothie)

Roasted Orange Juice

This recipe captured my imagination as a different take on a breakfast staple. It seems like roasting it wouldn't have a big impact on the flavor, but it really does taste very different once when the oranges are roasted. I love it, and I'm not normally a huge fan of OJ.

4 large oranges

1 c. water

¼ c. sugar

Optional Ingredients:

1 vanilla bean

Preheat oven to 350°F. Cut oranges in half and lay in a shallow roasting pan, cut sides up. Combine sugar and water and pour over the pan. Add the vanilla bean. Roast 25 minutes, until the orange slices start to caramelize. After cooling to room temperature, juice. Scrape seeds from the vanilla bean and whisk in, breaking up the seeds. Pour sugary water over a sieve and into the juice mixture. Whisk. Drink or refrigerate

Original Source: TarasMulticulturalTable.com (Roasted Vanilla Orange Juice)

Strawberry Lemonade

This is a favorite of my kids. My teenager gave it a rousing endorsement when I asked if I should make it again. He said, "Yeah, sure." Which, for a teenage boy, is a rousing endorsement indeed.

16 oz. strawberries or raspberries

Wash. Remove leaves from strawberries and cut into pieces. (Raspberries need to be washed but can go in whole.)

1½ c. sugar
2 liters water (approximately 8 c.)

Combine in a saucepan with the strawberries. Bring to a slow boil over medium-high. Lower to medium for 5-8 minutes. When strawberries are softened, cool to room temperature.

5 lemons (1 c. lemon juice)

Roll lemons firmly on the counter to make juicing easier, then juice. Mix all ingredients in a pitcher and refrigerate. You can adjust the amounts, and add fresh strawberries and lemons (cut into small pieces), to suit your taste.

Original Source: MyLatinaTable.com (Fresh Strawberry Lemonade)

Fizzy Lemonade

Add 4 c. (1 liter) of water when you boil the berries. Add a second 4 c. (1 liter) of club soda or selzer water to the finished drink.

Sweet Tea

The first time I made this, I wasn't sure what kind of tea we had on hand that would work best. I cut the recipe in half and made two 1 qt. batches, one with green tea and one with mint tea. It's easy to keep experimenting to find things he loves.

My youngest teen has a hard time waking up without caffeine. A soda every morning is not okay in my book (especially starting that young), so I wanted to find something else that's caffeinated, but not coffee because he doesn't like it. He does, however, love sweet tea and it occurred to me that in an emergency, there could be many people in the position of needing some caffeine but not liking coffee, so I hope you enjoy this Southern staple!

    2 c. boiling water

    6 tea bags (Lipton and Luzianne are favorites)

Pour boiling water in a 64 oz. glass pitcher (heat proof) and add tea bags. (I actually did that part in Pyrex measuring cups because I knew it was heatproof, and it was easy to get the teabags out.) Cover and steep for 5-15 minutes, depending on how strong you want the tea.

    ¾ c. sugar (to taste)

    6 c. cool water

Discard tea bags. Stir in sugar. When it's dissolved, pour in cool water and refrigerate until cold. Not just cool – cold. Serve over ice.

Optional Ingredients:

    A sprig of mint or a few lemon wedges

    A shot of bourbon or other liquor.

Any of these and many more things can be added for a little variety. You can also combine different kinds of tea to get the exact mix that works for your family.

9. Breakfast and Eggs

My family isn't big on breakfast, which is kind of ironic because we really enjoy breakfast food. On the weekend, we will happily all wake up and eat a nice brunch of waffles and bacon with syrup. It kind of makes sense since that's about the same time of day our breakfast-averse kids get lunch at school. We are naturals for brunch.

These are some of the recipes that we have enjoyed the most, and a few that take advantage of ingredients you may need to use up, like cottage cheese. (I know I'm not the only one who has the best of intentions for eating healthy when starting a new container of cottage cheese.)

Quiche feels like a grown-up way to enjoy eggs beyond breakfast. Frittata's are similar to a quiche but without the crust, and with the added benefit of being good in a sandwich. Deviled Eggs are a classic appetizer, something we all need sometimes, and this unusual twist can help you use up that package of cream cheese you bought, right before you forgot to pick up bagels. Eggs can serve as breakfast, lunch, or dinner. Eggs are flexible.

Several recipes need egg whites whipped to form stiff peaks. I recommend reading theSpruceEats.com post on "All About Whipping Egg Whites" if you don't already know how. If you really want to explore all the ways to make eggs, there is a YouTube™ "Every Way to Cook an Egg (59 Methods)" from Bon Appetit that gives an incredibly quick overview of cooking eggs.

Eggs (and dairy, among other things) can cause constipation if you eat too many of them, especially if you mix in cheese, unless you make sure to eat enough fiber to counter the tendency toward constipation. They are, of course, a good source of protein. Just something to keep in mind!

Almond Flour Pancakes

On the lookout for healthier alternatives, we found almond flour pancakes, which were surprisingly tasty and diabetic-friendly.

>   2¼ c. blanched almond flour
>
>   4 eggs
>
>   1 c. water or milk (adjust to desired thickness)

Optional Ingredients:

>   cinnamon, nutmeg, vanilla, blueberries

Mix all ingredients. Cook 2-3 minutes per side, until bubbles form and pancakes are golden brown.

Bacon, Oven Baked

It's amazing the places we learn things today. While playing a Wii cooking game, I learned that it is possible to make bacon in the oven. No more splattering bacon grease! It's also easier to make the rest of the meal at the same time.

>   Bacon

Bake at 375°F for 15 minutes in a jelly roll or other pan with an edge to prevent the grease from dripping off the edges. If you put the bacon on a cooling tray (the kind you use to cool muffins or bread) inside the pan, the bacon ends up crispier and less greasy.

Breakfast Quesadilla

I almost didn't include this because it sounded so...unusual, but it is quite tasty and a great way to use up a small amount of berries.

  2 small flour tortillas
  1-2 Tbsp. peanut butter
  Handful of berries
  10 chocolate chips (approximate)

Grease a pan and heat over medium. Spread peanut butter on both tortillas. Put berries on top of one tortilla, then top with chocolate chips. Put the second tortilla on top, peanut butter side down. Cook 2-3 minutes per side, until lightly browned, then flip and repeat. When both sides are lightly browned, slice and enjoy

Original Source: ACultivatedNest.com (Healthy Breakfast Quesadilla)

Breakfast Parfait

I love things that are easy to tailor to personal preferences and what's available. This is a perfect example of that.

  ¼ c. granola, nuts, or crushed crackers
  ¼ c. yogurt
  ¼ c. fruit or berries

For the fruit, you can use berry compote, cranberry sauce, roasted peaches/apricots, or jelly/jam if fresh berries aren't available. Layer the three ingredients in a cup or mug. Mix them when you eat.

Cottage Cheese Pancakes

  4 egg whites
  ½ c. oats
  ¼ c. cottage cheese

Mix all ingredients. Cook like a pancake. Top with jelly, applesauce, or even berry compote.

Original Source: Facebook (thanks Cindy and Andrea!)

Crepes

These are another great way to use whatever is on hand. But mostly, I really love crepes, and this recipe in particular.

> 1 c. flour
> 1 c. milk
> 3 eggs
> 1 tsp. butter

Stir flour and eggs. Slowly add in milk. Heat a crepe pan or skillet over medium. Melt butter to coat the pan. Pour 2 Tbsp. of batter into the center, then tilt pan to spread the batter evenly. Return to heat and cook 1-2 minutes, until it is golden underneath. Flip and cook another 1-2 minutes. Transfer to a plate and fill with whatever you heart desires, sweet or savory. Filling options include:

> Scrambled eggs and veggies
> Fruit and berries
> Cheese

Original Source: an elementary school friend's German mother (thanks Liz!)

Deviled Eggs

The traditional recipe calls for mayonnaise but I enjoy the smooth texture cream cheese (especially homemade) provides.

> 12 hard-boiled eggs, peeled
> 1 (8 oz.) package cream cheese (or flavored) OR ½ c. mayonnaise
> 1 tsp. paprika

Cut eggs in half length-wise and scoop the yolks out into a bowl. Put the whites on a plate with the empty space up. Mash yolks with a fork and add cream cheese (or mayo). Mix well. Spoon yolk mixture into the empty space and sprinkle with paprika, if desired. Refrigerate twenty minutes before eating. You can also mix in or top with other ingredients such as fresh ground pepper, bacon bits, onion, garlic, ranch dressing, hot sauce, lemon juice, mustard, and avocado.

Original Source: Allrecipes.com (Creamy Deviled Eggs, Epicurean Deviled Eggs)

Ebelskiver (Pancake Puffs)

My son was determined to get the "Pancake Puff Maker", which I found out basically makes Ebelskiver, a traditional Danish dessert

> 1¼ c. all-purpose flour
> 3 Tbsp. sugar
> 2¾ tsp. baking powder
> ¼ tsp. ground cardamom
> ¼ tsp. salt
> 1 large egg
> 1 c. milk
> 2 Tbsp. melted butter

Optional Fillings:

> jam/preserves
> pudding, honey
> chocolate

Mix flour, sugar, baking powder, cardamom, and salt. Separately, mix egg, milk, and butter. Stir into flour mixture until evenly moistened. Heat pan on medium-low until a drop of water dances on it. Brush cups lightly with melted butter. Spoon batter to slightly below the rim. For filled ebelskiver, pour in about 1 tsp. of batter. Drop ½ tsp. of filling into the center. Fill with batter to slightly below the rim. Adjust filling/batter ratio to taste. In about 90 seconds, thin crusts will form on the bottom. Pierce with a skewer and rotate 90 degrees so half the new top is cooked and batter flows down. In 60 seconds, repeat so the entire original bottom is now on top. Continue to turn periodically until balls are fully cooked, 10-12 minutes. If balls get too brown, lower heat until they are cooked in the center. Serve hot.

Original Source: As Seen on TV

Egg-a-muffin Sandwich

Fast, easy, and cheap. What's not to love?

1 Tbsp. butter

2 large eggs

Heat butter over medium in a skillet. Lightly oil 2 Mason jar lid rings and put them in the pan, or use egg molds. Break the eggs into a bowl, whisk gently, and pour into rings. Cook 3-4 minutes, covered. Eggs should be cooked through before removing from the heat and the rings.

1 Tbsp. mayonnaise

1-2 sausage patties OR canned ham

1-2 slices cheese

Avocado slices

The eggs will be the "bread" for this sandwich. Put them on a plate. Spread half of the mayo on each egg. Put the sausage patty on one egg and top with a slice of cheese. Repeat if you are using two sausage patties and slices of cheese. Top with avocado, then the final egg. If you use canned ham, slice to about the thickness of sausage patties, then use a canning ring to slice it into a circle.

Original Source: PeaceLoveAndLowCarb.com (Keto Sausage and Egg Breakfast Sandwich)

Eggs (Pasteurized)

This can be made with a sous vide or a WAPI.

Eggs

Water

Put eggs in 135°F water for 45 minutes. There is no need for a bag since they have a shell. They will be uncooked and ready to use for any recipe that calls for eggs. If you are making anything that requires whipping stiff peaks from the egg white, you may need to add cream of tartar or lemon juice. Otherwise, they can be used like non-pasteurized eggs without the risk of salmonella. Some grocery store eggs are already pasteurized.

Eggy Muffin Cups

I made these using silicone muffin cups, paper muffin cups, and just in the greased pan. The paper cups were an utter fail. The batter is too liquid. The silicone ones were the easiest to use. The eggs did stick a bit to the metal pan. I recommend never using paper muffin cups for this recipe.

> 6 eggs

Optional Ingredients:

> ⅓ c. cooked bacon, crumbled
>
> ⅓ c. shredded cheddar cheese

Preheat oven to 375°F. Lightly butter 6 standard muffin cups. Whisk eggs until smooth. Add remaining ingredients and stir. Divide among muffin cups. Bake 15-18 minutes, until eggs are set.

Original Source: DinnerAtTheZoo.com (Breakfast Egg Muffins)

French Toast Sticks

These are one of my kids' favorites. Now I don't "need" to buy frozen ones! Since French toast is best with stale bread, I also have a use for that now. Double woot!

The original recipe called for frying these in 2 quarts of vegetable oil. I avoid frying whenever possible for health reasons, and because grease splatters. In an emergency, using that much oil just for frying is incredibly wasteful. If you prefer fried, you can go back to the original recipe online for those instructions.

> ½ c. sugar
>
> 2 Tsp. cinnamon

Combine and set topping aside.

> 2 c. milk
>
> ¼ c. sugar
>
> 2 eggs
>
> ½ tsp. salt

½ tsp. vanilla

Whisk together until smooth

1 c. flour

2 tsp. baking powder

Add to liquid and mix until smooth and lump-free.

8 slices thick bread (or Texas Toast)

Pre-heat skillet over medium heat. Cut each slice of bread into 4 strips. I prefer adding the cinnamon sugar to the batter before cooking, but you can roll the baked French toast sticks in the cinnamon sugar, if you prefer. Either add it to the batter or set it to the side.

Dip a few bread sticks at a time in the batter, allowing any extra to drip back, then cook until golden brown, 2-3 minutes. When the first side is golden brown, flip and cook the second side. If you set the cinnamon sugar to the side, roll French toast sticks in the topping immediately after removing them from the heat.

If you won't eat them for 10-20 minutes or so: Preheat the oven to 200°F. Line a cookie sheet with parchment paper or a silpat. Put sticks on the baking sheet in the oven to keep them warm until eaten.

To freeze and reheat: Freeze on a tray. Move to an airtight container. Reheat 7-10 minutes in a 400°F oven or microwave 1 minute.

Original Source: CulinaryHill.com (French Toast Sticks)

Frittata

This is a great way to use leftovers.

4 eggs

¼ c. milk

¼ tsp. dried herb such as rosemary

Salt and pepper

2 tsp. butter

½-1 cup filling

Thoroughly whisk all ingredients except filling and butter. Add in the filling, whatever vegetables, fruit, and cheese you have on hand. Melt butter in a frying pan over medium heat. Cook mixture until eggs are almost set. Remove from heat and cover so it continues cooking. In 5-10 minutes, there shouldn't be any more visible liquid and it will be ready to eat.

To make them in muffin cups, preheat oven to 350°F. Grease a 12 cup muffin pan. Heat 1 Tbsp. butter and filling ingredients in a skillet over medium heat for 6-8 minutes. Whisk ingredients together and fill each muffin cup almost to the top. Bake until top is lightly golden, about 15 minutes. Cool 2 minutes. These are easy to carry.

Original Source: IncredibleEgg.com

Hard Boiled Eggs

> Eggs

Put eggs in a pot and cover fully with water. Bring to a boil. Reduce heat and simmer 10 minutes. Refrigerate until needed. If yolk edges turn green, it is overcooked. Shorten the time until it is perfect.

Lemon-Ricotta Dutch Baby

I had never heard of a "Dutch Baby" before I started writing cookbooks. This old German specialty is sort of a large pancake and there are many variations.

> ¾ c. flour
>
> ¼ c. sugar
>
> ½ tsp. baking powder
>
> ¼ tsp. salt

Preheat oven to 425°F. Put a 12" cast iron pan inside to preheat. Whisk ingredients to combine.

> 1 c. milk
>
> 5 eggs
>
> ⅓ c. ricotta
>
> 1 lemon – juice and zest

½ tsp. vanilla

Blend ingredients until smooth, then add to dry ingredients. Whisk until just combined. When I used homemade ricotta, it was a bit clumpy. Breaking up the clumps sped up the process.

2 Tbsp. butter

½ c. raspberries and blueberries

Remove skillet and put butter in it. Stir until melted, then add batter. Sprinkle berries on top. Bake 10 minutes. Center will be set and edges will be golden brown.

Original Source: BarbaraBakes.com (Deer Valley Lemon Ricotta Dutch Baby)

Mexicorn Grits

Mexicorn is corn kernals mixed with a smaller amount of red and green peppers, with some spices mixed in. There is a recipe for it on page 149.

4 c. milk

½ c. butter

Combine and bring to a boil.

1 c. grits

Stir in grits. Reduce heat. Cook and stir 5-7 minutes.

2 large eggs

Whisk. Stir in about 2 Tbsp. grits to temper eggs. Return to pan.

⅓ c. butter

Melt butter and stir in.

1 can (11 oz.) Mexicorn, drained (or 1½ c. fresh Mexicorn)

1 can (4 oz.) chopped green chillies

1 c. shredded Mexican cheese blend

1 tsp. salt

¼ tsp. white pepper.

Preheat oven to 350°F. Grease a 2 qt. baking dish. Add all ingredients except Parmesan cheese and pour into baking dish.

> 1 c. shredded Parmesan cheese

Sprinkle with Parmesan. Bake uncovered for 35-40 minutes. Knife inserted in the center will come out clean when it is finished.

Original Source: TasteOfHome.com (Mexicorn Grits)

Pickled Eggs

I was kind of torn about where to put these. They are a spring classic in the area where I grew up and can be eaten any time of day. Breakfast? Of course! Snack? Obviously. Side dish with lunch or dinner? Duh. Whatever meal you think they go with, enjoy! And no, you don't have to eat the beets, although in some families they are the favorite part.

If you grew up in an area with pickled eggs, you almost certainly saw them in a jar on the counter (or in the pantry on *Roseanne*), not in a refrigerator. This is _not_ recommended today. Home-pickled eggs should stay refrigerated until you are ready to eat them.

> 1½ dozen hard-boiled eggs
> 2 cans of beets
> ¾ c. vinegar
> ½ c. sugar

Put beet juice, vinegar, and sugar in a pot. Mix. Heat until the sugar melts. Put peeled eggs and beets in a container, being sure to mix them up and not layer them. Glass is best because I think beets can stain just about anything, but is not necessary. Store the container in the refrigerator for at least twenty-four hours before they are done.

Finished, these pickled eggs range from pink to purple. How dark and how far through the color goes is in part related to how long it's in the beet/vinegar solution.

Original Source: Aunt Blue

Potato Pancakes

Potato pancakes are a food I know I ate periodically growing up but I can't remember any particular time I ate them. I love them, especially with applesauce on top, but I think I may be the only on in the family. That means more potato pancakes for me!

> 2 c. mashed potatoes
>
> 2 Tbsp. flour
>
> 1 egg

You can use boxed mashed potatoes if you don't have any mashed potatoes on hand. You can also bake enough potatoes to yield approximately 2 c. potatoes and add 4 oz. milk. (Mashed potatoes are basically potato + milk.) Mix all ingredients except butter and form into patties.

> 2 Tbsp. butter

Melt butter in a frying pan over medium heat. Drop batter in by rounded tablespoons and fry for three minutes, then flatten slightly with the spatula, if needed, and flip. Fry an additional three minutes and flip again. They should be golden brown on both sides. They are traditionally topped with applesauce.

Protein Pancakes

> 1⅓ c. rolled oats
>
> 1 tsp. baking powder

Blend until the consistency of flour. Set aside in a bowl.

> ½ c. cottage cheese
>
> 2 large eggs
>
> ½ c. water
>
> 1 tsp. olive oil
>
> 1 tsp. vanilla
>
> Dash of cinnamon

Grease and preheat griddle. Combine remaining ingredients in the blender and blend until smooth. Add dry ingredients and blend. Pour

¼ c. per pancake onto hot griddle. Cook until you see bubbles on top, then flip and cook until golden

Original Source: TastesBetterFromScratch.com (Protein Pancakes)

Quiche

You can make a homemade pie crust, but if you use a store crust, this is a fast and easy meal. Like frittatas, this is a good way to use small amounts of veggies and such. Bonus: you can put different fillings in different parts, which can be huge if you have picky kids.

> 1 pie crust (frozen or homemade)
>
> 6 eggs
>
> ¾ c. milk
>
> ½ c. grated cheese or 2 oz. crumbled goat cheese

Optional Filling Ingredients (pick and choose as your health allows):

> Salt and pepper to taste
>
> 3 Tbsp. onions
>
> 1c. cooked meat
>
> 1 chopped pepper
>
> 4 c. mixed greens
>
> ⅛ tsp. nutmeg
>
> ½ c. grated cheese

If you use any kind of vegetables in the filling, partially pre-cook them in a skillet to ensure they are fully and completely cooked before you eat them. People without allergy or histamine issues can skip this step.

Preheat oven to 375°F. Press pie crust into a 9" pie plate. Whisk milk and eggs. Scatter optional ingredients on the pie crust and top with egg mixture. Sprinkle cheese on top. Bake 35-40 minutes. Center will be completely set. Cool 5-10 minutes before slicing.

Original Source: SpendWithPennies.com (How to Make Easy Quiche)

Rice Eggs (Tamago Gohan)

This is fast and easy to make. With little more than rice and an egg, it's very easy on the tummy and provides some protein. The original recipe specifically recommended basmati rice, but my family prefers jasmine and many people choose brown rice for health reasons. Use your favorite rice, or whatever is on hand. Personally, this is far more than I want in one meal. Sometimes I add meatballs, a bit of stir fry, or other leftovers, which is a good approach for lunch or dinner. I'm a huge fan of flexible recipes like this.

> ½ c. uncooked rice
>
> 1 c. water

Combine and boil. Cover and simmer 10 minutes

> 1 egg
>
> 1 tsp. soy sauce

As soon as the rice is done, put it in a bowl. Crack the egg over the rice and combine them. Add soy sauce. You can let it set 5-10 minutes to thicken. Heat from the rice will slightly cook the egg, similar to an over-easy egg. You can also heat it for another 30 seconds or use a pasteurized egg (instructions on page 109) to further reduce the risk of salmonella.

Original Source: SusansTable.com (Japanese Breakfast Rice Bowl)

Scrambled Eggs

A TV show recommended adding butter to scrambled eggs and my teens strongly prefer it this way, so it's going in my cookbook!

> Eggs
>
> 1 Tbsp. butter per two eggs

Optional Ingredients:

> Soft, young cheese

Simple is best. Put the eggs and butter in together, then scramble the eggs. Melt in cheese just before they finish, if desired.

10. Sandwiches and Bread

Bread is a staple around the world and this selection of recipes shows that: bagels, naan, tortillas, and more. It goes beyond what most of us think in terms of "bread", especially when used in the same sentence as sandwich. In addition, you can make your own with oat or rye flour, depending on what you have available. Generally speaking, "quick breads" rely more on baking powder than yeast, even in box mixes, which gives you options if you are out of yeast. These are easy to make and easily altered to match your food needs.

Bread sometimes needs to rise in a warm space, which can be tough in the winter. If you run into this issue and your house doesn't have anywhere particularly warm, set your oven to "warm." Allow it to heat up for five minutes before turning it off. Open the door and let the dough rest in the open, warm oven. Make sure you don't heat the oven so much that you heat or melt the container the dough is in. The goal is to simulate a warm summer window, not bake anything. In cold weather, a Wonderbag could be a good place to let bread dough rise.

You can put an egg wash (page84) on many kinds of bread. It's basically eggs and some water that make it have a nice finish.

Applesauce Bread

Every parent has gotten stuck with a bunch of something their child *loved* and ate non-stop, right up until they didn't. This nicely uses up one six-pack of individual applesauce packs. It also creates a healthy, moist loaf of bread.

> 4 eggs, room temperature
> 1½ c. sugar

Combine. It should thicken and turn yellow, about the color of lemons.

> 3 c. applesauce, room temperature
> 2 sticks butter, melted and slightly cooled

Add to mixture, being sure to scrape down the bowl sides. It may seem curdled but that is normal.

> 3 c. flour
> 1 Tbsp. baking soda
> 1 tsp. kosher salt
> ½ tsp. cinnamon

Combine. Add to mixture.

> Optional:
> 2 c. walnuts

Preheat oven to 350°F. Add nuts, if desired. Pour into loaf or muffin pans. Bake bread for about one hour, muffins for 20-25 minutes. It will be golden brown when done. Cool 5 minutes, then move to a wire rack to finish cooling.

Original Source: LeitesCulinaria.com (Applesauce Bread)

Bagels

My husband says these taste biscuit-like, but they are fast and easy, and don't require boiling, and this book is about simple recipes. Personally, I like them.

> 1c. flour

2 tsp baking powder

¾ tsp. kosher salt

Combine and whisk well.

1 c. Greek yogurt (the thicker consistency is important)

Preheat oven to 375°F. Add yogurt to flour mixture until it looks like crumbles. Flour a work surface. Knead dough on it until dough is tacky but not sticky, 15-20 turns, sprinkling more flour on if dough becomes sticky. When you pull your hand away, the dough should not stick to it. Split into 3 equal pieces. Roll each into a ¾" thick rope. Form each rope into a bagel. You can also make a ball, poke a hole in the center, then stretch it a bit to make the hole bigger.

Optional Egg Wash Ingredients:

1 egg white or whole egg

2 Tbsp. water

Pinch salt

Beat the egg white. Add remaining ingredients. Brush on top of bagels. Add toppings (cheese, sesame seeds, etc.), if desired. Bake on top rack for 25 minutes. Cool at least 15 minutes before cutting.

Original Source: SkinnyTaste.com (Easy Bagel Recipe)

Bagel Balls

The apple dip in chapter 5 of this book is a very tasty filling for these, but it is mostly cream cheese.

Bagel dough (previous recipe)

4 Tbsp. cream cheese or other filling

Preheat oven to 375°F. Make bagel dough (previous recipe). Divide into 4 parts, then roll into balls. Form each one into a deep bowl and fill with about 1 Tbsp. cream cheese. Pinch the edges closed to seal them. Put parchment paper on a cookie sheet and balls on the cookie sheet. Bake 15-20 minutes. Some of the filling will be absorbed by the dough.

You can vary it by adding herbs, spices, etc. to the cream cheese. Apple Dip (page 81) makes a very tasty filling.

Banana Bread

I made this with oat flour instead of wheat flour and it turned out really well. Oat flour can make things dry so you often need to use a bit less of it than you would with wheat flour, but the bananas are so moist you can simply do 2 c. oat flour instead of 2 c. wheat.

> 2 c. flour
> 1 tsp. baking soda
> ¼ tsp. salt
> ½ c. butter
> ¾ c. brown sugar
> 2 eggs
> 2⅓ c. overripe bananas

Preheat oven to 350°F. Lightly grease a 9x5 loaf pan. Beat the eggs. Mash the bananas. Combine flour, baking soda, and salt. In another bowl, cream butter and brown sugar. Stir in eggs and bananas until well blended. Combine all the ingredients in one bowl and stir until just moistened. Pour into loaf pan and bake 60-65 minutes. Let cool in pan for ten minutes.

Beer Bread

You can use any carbonated beverage in beer bread. That means you can use soda or sparkling water, which gives you a lot more options. The original recipe called for 3 c. flour, which I found made the bread far too dense but if you like very dense bread, increase the flour to 3 c. If this is still denser than you like, decrease it to 2 c.

> 1 (12 oz.) can beer, soda, or sparkling water
> 2½ c. self-rising flour, sifted
> 3 Tbsp. sugar

Optional Ingredients:

> ¼-½ c. butter

Preheat oven to 350°F. Combine dry ingredients, then add beer/soda. For a softer crust, add optional butter into the batter now. Grease a loaf pan and pour the mixture in. Bake for 50-60 minutes, then cool for at least 15 minutes before eating.

Breadsticks

> 2½ c. medium hot water
>
> 5 tsp. instant yeast OR 2 Tbsp. regular yeast

Pour water in a mixing bowl and sprinkle with yeast. Don't stir. Allow yeast to dissolve.

> 2 Tbsp. sugar
>
> 3 Tbsp. oil
>
> 1 tsp. salt
>
> 6 c. whole wheat flour*
>
> * Half whole wheat and half all-purpose flour works too.

Add sugar, salt, and oil after the yeast has dissolved. Combine. Gradually add flour. Preheat oven to 400°F. Roll dough into ½-1" wide length and cut to length for breadsticks. Lay breadsticks on the tray. Sprinkle with cheese and herbs to taste or baste with butter, if desired. Cook 10-12 minutes or until cheese (if used) is slightly browned. They will rise and become firm. You can also form them into rolls or loaves.

Cinnamon Swirl Bread

You can substitute other spices for cinnamon, if desired.

> ⅓ c. sugar
>
> 2 tsp. cinnamon (or substitute another spice)

In a small bowl, mix the sugar and cinnamon.

> 2 c. flour
>
> 1 tsp. baking powder
>
> ½ tsp. salt
>
> 1 c. sugar

1 egg

1 c. milk

⅓ c. vegetable oil

Preheat oven to 350°F. Lightly grease a 9x5 loaf pan. Beat egg. In a larger bowl, combine flour, baking powder, salt, and sugar. Mix egg, milk, and oil and add to dry ingredients. Stir until just moistened.

Pour half the batter into the loaf pan. Sprinkle with half the sugar mixture. Repeat with the other half of the batter and sugar mixes. Draw a knife through the batter to create a marble pattern. Bake 45-50 minutes. Let cool 10 minutes before removing to a wire rack to finish cooling. Wrap in foil and let set overnight before slicing.

Cornbread

In my cookbooks, I abbreviate tablespoon as Tbsp. and teaspoon as tsp. but there are a few variations on those around, particularly not capitalizing tablespoon. The original from this cornbread recipe, however, used tspn for teaspoon and tbspn for tablespoon. When I transcribed the recipe, I wrote Tbsp. instead of tsp. for everything! To make matters even worse, I used corn starch instead of corn meal. That bread came out a flat, dense, salty mess! And I went back to re-read the original and find out where I went wrong.

The second try? Perfect. Absolutely perfect! And it was great in the Church Soup I made while it baked.

¾ c. corn meal

1 c. flour

1½ Tbsp. sugar

1 tsp. baking soda

1 tsp. cream of tartar

1 tsp. salt

Sift together

1 egg

Beat egg.

2 Tbsp. butter, melted

1 c. sour cream

4 Tbsp. milk

Preheat oven to 425°F. Add egg and other remaining ingredients to dry mix. Beat well. Grease a 9" bread pan and pour batter into it. Bake for 20 minutes.

Original Source: CrackingGoodEgg.blogspot.com (Amish Sour Cream Corn Bread)

Grilled Cheese with Chutney

Of course you can always make a regular grilled cheese with American cheese (Cooper is the best brand) on a griddle, but this slightly fancier version is a nice change of pace. It's also surprisingly fast and easy to make. Since this is baked, not grilled, the outside won't be golden brown like most grilled cheese.

2 slices bread

2 Tbsp. olive oil or butter

Heat griddle or non-stick skillet over medium heat. Baste outside of each slice of bread with olive oil or butter.

1 Tbsp. chutney

2 slices Gouda cheese

4-6 thin apple slices (optional)

Place first slice of bread oil-side down in skillet. Layer cheese slice, chutney, apple slices (if desired), cheese slice, and bread (oil side up) on top of the first slice of bread. Bake 3 minutes. Flip. Cook 3 more minutes. Both sides should be golden brown and cheese should be melted.

Original Source: Sargento.com (Grilled Cheese 3 Ways)

Lemon Zucchini Bread

My two year old didn't like vegetables, but he loved his Aunt Blue's zucchini bread so much that she mailed frozen loaves halfway across North America to him. I like this twist on it.

1½ c. flour

½ tsp. baking soda

¼ tsp. baking powder

¼ tsp. salt

Combine. Set aside.

¾ c. sugar

1 c. unpeeled zucchini, grated (do not squeeze or dry)

¼ c. cooking oil

1 egg

2 Tbsp. lemon juice

2 Tbsp. lemon zest

Preheat oven to 350°F. Grease a bread pan. Combine wet ingredients. Stir in dry ingredients until just combined, then spoon into greased pan. Bake 50-55 minutes, until golden brown and set. Cool 15 minutes on a wire rack before removing from pan and cooling completely. Must be completely cool before drizzling the glaze on.

½ c. powdered sugar

1 Tbsp. lemon juice

1 tsp. lemon zest

Combine and drizzle over cooled bread. Stores well frozen.

Naan

We really love this recipe. It's also great with herbs on top.

2 c. flour

3 tsp. sugar

1 tsp. fast-rising yeast (NOT regular yeast)

Mix dry ingredients.

¾ c. water

2 Tbsp. olive oil

3 Tbsp. yogurt (Greek yogurt works)

Mix moist ingredients separately from dry. Combine both in one bowl until the dough just sticks together. Flour your hands and form it into a ball, then flour the outside of the ball. Grease the inside of a bowl large enough to allow the dough ball to double in size. Put the dough in the bowl and cover with cling wrap or a damp kitchen towel, then put it in a warm place to rise. In ninety minutes, it should have doubled in size and be ready to cook, but it may take longer.

Heat a non-stick skillet or iron frying pan on medium-high. Put dough on a floured rolling board and roll into a rectangle. Cut the rectangle into six equal pieces, which you will roll into six balls. Flour each of the six dough balls and put them to the side. Roll one out into a roughly circular shape. Turn the heat down to medium and put the first dough in the skillet. In 2-3 minutes, you should see bubbles on top of the naan. More bubbles generally equals more well-cooked. When you are satisfied with the number of bubbles, flip it over and cook for another 2-3 minutes. Remove and cook the next one.

You can brush olive oil or butter on top before you flip it. You can also add garlic, rosemary, oregano, or another herb to the top.

Pa-SPAM®-mi Sandwich

SPAM gets a bad rap but a lot of people must like it or it wouldn't be in so many grocery stores. It's easy to keep on hand and has a *very* long shelf life.

>   2 French rolls
>
>   4 slices provolone or other desired cheese

Preheat oven to 375°F. Put 2 slices of cheese on the top half of each roll. Bake on a baking sheet 5 minutes or until cheese melts.

>   1 can SPAM (12 oz.) or canned ham
>
>   ½ tsp. ground coriander or ginger
>
>   ¼ c. prepared yellow mustard

Shred SPAM using the large holes on a cheese grater. Put spices on SPAM and fry on medium-high until brown, about 5 minutes. Spread

1 Tbsp. mustard on each half of the rolls. Put half of cooked SPAM on each roll, close, and serve.

Pocket Sandwich

I remember these from Scout trip campfires. Now, you can buy a gadget to make them in the house, but they remain a great emergency option if you make them over a campfire.

> 2 slices bread per sandwich
> Filling: peanut butter and jelly, just jelly, or meat and cheese

Put the fillings on one slice of bread and top with the second slice, being careful to allow space at the edge so it doesn't spill out. Put the stuffed sandwich on either an electric hot pocket maker or use one designed to go over an open fire.

Ramen Burger Bun

When it comes to emergency food, nothing is cheaper or more widely available than that college staple, ramen noodles. Recently, there has been a surge in new ways to use that old favorite, such as by creating burger buns with it. It's a fun twist on it!

1 package ramen noodles

Set aside the seasoning packet (it isn't needed unless you want seasoned buns) and cook following the package instructions.

1 egg

Beat egg. Drain and rinse the noodles. Stir in the beaten egg. Divide noodles in half. (If you prefer thinner buns, divide noodles in four parts.) Grease two ramekins or small bowls, or spray with cooking spray. Cover tightly with cling wrap and weigh down with canned goods to ensure noodles are tightly packed together. Refrigerate a minimum of 15 minutes, but it can be a few days.

Cooking oil

Cook on a hot, greased skillet over medium heat. Cook 2-3 minutes. When the bottom is golden brown, flip and repeat.

SANDWICHES AND BREAD

Original Source: SpoonUniversity.com (Make a Ramen Burger at Home)

Sliders

>1 lb. ground turkey
>
>6 slices cheese
>
>1 package slider buns

Put a greased grill pan on low-medium heat. Form ground turkey into patties about half the size of a regular hamburger, adding a dash of salt and pepper or other spices, if desired. Cook for approximately 10 minutes, flipping halfway through, making sure to cook thoroughly. Add toppings based on your preferences.

Grocery stores now carry smaller slider buns in addition to regular size burger buns.

S'mores Sandwich

This is just full of yummy goodness. Too bad it isn't also full of health and nutrition. (It should probably be under "desserts".)

>Nutella
>
>Marshmallow Fluff
>
>Bread

Put Nutella and Marshmallow Fluff each on a piece of bread. Smash together and eat.

Stuffing (Matzo)

It's easy to customize stuffing by adding whatever veggies and spices you have on hand, even using add-ins like bacon.

>Olive oil
>
>1 carrot, diced
>
>1 apple, diced
>
>1 12-14 oz. box matzo
>
>4 c. broth (chicken, turkey, vegetable, etc.)*
>
>2 eggs, lightly beaten
>
>2 sticks butter

Pinch garlic powder

Salt and pepper to taste

*Chapter 10 has a recipe for homemade chicken broth.

Preheat oven to 375°F. Break matzo into pieces. Sauté carrots and apples in olive oil until they are soft, about 10-12 minutes. Add matzo and toast it for two minutes before adding spices and anything else you want to add in. Grease a 9x13 dish. Dump matzo mixture into a large bowl and add the broth and eggs, then melted butter. Put mixture in the dish. Bake uncovered 45 minutes or until browned.

Original Source: JustaPinch.com (Matzo Stuffing)

Tortillas (Corn)

2½ c. corn flour

½ c. vegetable shortening

1 tsp. salt

1¼ c. water

Mix all ingredients until smooth. It shouldn't stick to your hands or flake apart. If it's too dry, add water ½ tsp. at a time. If it's sticky, add flour ½ tsp. at a time. Make 2" balls of dough and flatten them into a circle. (Larger or smaller balls will result in larger or smaller finished tortillas.) Cook on a dry griddle or frying pan with oil.

11. Soup

Watching the leaves falling and the temperature dropping may have impacted my choice to dedicate a chapter to soup, the ultimate cold weather comfort food. It's also the best comfort food when we are sick. In an emergency, we may not have the same options for ready-made food. Even the soups that sound bland (like oatmeal soup) are still warm and filling. Slow cookers are an outstanding way to both make soup and ensure fruits and veggies are very well cooked, which is important if they were close to going bad.

Soup can easily be cooked in advance and frozen. Chicken soup, in particular, is good for sick days and can be made in advance for sick days later. Soups can also be made in advance and frozen if you have advance notice of a potential emergency, like a large storm, so you don't lose as much of your food. Cooked food stays safe to eat longer than raw food (protein in particular) and frozen food stays safe to eat longer than refrigerated.

Comparison: Broth, Stock, and Bouillon

For professional chefs, the differences are important. For purposes of this cookbook, I use them interchangeably and you can too. Broth and stock have slightly different ingredients and cook times. Stock always has added bones and doesn't have any added spices. Broth contains meat but doesn't necessarily have bones, and usually has added spices and aromatics including garlic, carrots, and onion. Broth isn't cooked for as many hours as stock. Because it has fewer ingredients, stock may be easier to make if you have limited ingredients on hand.

Bouillon cubes are a dehydrated, concentrated paste preserved with salt, making them crazy high in salt, but they can be handy and they have a very, very long shelf life. I used them for Matzo Ball soup because I had no broth at home. Bouillon is also very cheap and long-lasting, making it easy to keep on hand. You can make your own broth, stock, and bouillon but I haven't found a recipe for bouillon that I can eat with my specific allergies.

Berry Soup

Cold berry soup is a lovely summer treat. Blended and chilled, it's very close to a smoothie and I have been known to drink it.

> ½ c. barley
> 6 c. water

Soak overnight in water. Simmer over low heat for 1 hour.

> ½ c. sugar
> 10 oz. frozen raspberries
> ½ c. raisins

Add and simmer for another 30 minutes.

> 1 c. pitted cherries

Add cherries and simmer for a final 15 minutes or until it thickens. Blend, if desired. Chill. Blended, it can also be drunk like a smoothie.

Butternut Squash Soup

This is one of my favorite fall recipes.

> 1-1½ lbs. butternut squash
> 1 Tbsp. butter (unsalted)
> 3 c. chicken broth

Pepper, nutmeg, ginger, or cinnamon to taste

Peel, seed, and cut butternut squash into 1" chunks. Melt butter in a pot large enough to hold all ingredients. Mix in squash and broth. Simmer until the squash is fully cooked and tender/ready to fall apart. It should take about twenty minutes. Puree chunks of squash in a blender. Return to pot and add spices.

Optional Ingredients:

4 Tbsp. peanut powder OR 2 Tbsp. peanut butter

For a twist, you can add peanut powder or peanut butter to make **Peanut Butternut Squash Soup**.

Cheddar Cheese Soup

> 2 c. milk
> 2 c. half and half or chicken broth

Heat the milk and half and half or broth over medium to medium-high heat.

> 4 Tbsp. butter
> ½ c. sifted flour
> ½ tsp. dry mustard

Melt butter. Whisk in flour and other ingredients. Cook over medium until it thickens and simmers.

> 1½ c. cheddar cheese
> ¼ tsp. salt
> ¼ tsp. pepper

Dice cheese or use shredded. Stir in until just melted. Add salt and pepper to taste.

Cherry Soup

The first time I made it, I simply blended sour cream and a <u>unsweetened</u> pie mix, then chilled. It was similar to flavored yogurt. I finally found the sour cherries in cherry juice (not pie mix) in another part of the store, with employee help.

1 can (16 oz.) pitted sour red pie cherries

1½ tsp. cornstarch

½ c. cold water

Drain juice from cherries into a medium sauce pan. Set cherries aside. Combine cornstarch and water, then add to juice. Heat to boiling and boil for 5 minutes, stirring constantly.

1 Tbsp. sugar

2 Tbsp. lemon juice

Add sugar and lemon juice. Stir, remove from heat, and chill.

1 c. sour cream

Blend sour cream and drained cherries. Add to juice mix. Chill well. It is nice served in chilled cups, or drunk like a smoothie.

Chicken Broth

A lot of recipes use chicken and other kinds of broth. Knowing how to make your own can make a huge difference in an emergency.

1 lb. chicken parts

1 parsnip

6 c. water

Garlic to taste

Onion to taste

Put all ingredients in a large pot. Bring to a boil, then lower heat. Cover and simmer for one hour. Remove chicken parts. Skim fat from the surface*, then strain stock through cheesecloth.

*The matzo ball soup recipe in this chapter uses skimmed fat, so keep it if you plan to make that.

Chicken and Bean Soup

This recipe is Exhibit One in why cookbook writers have to make every single recipe. This was actually a recipe for chili but the final result was absolutely soupy. Having a fairly minimal background in all things cooking, I used butter beans in this recipe since they are, in fact, pretty much white, which could be the reason it didn't turn out like chili. (It turns out that navy, Great Northern, cannellini, and baby lima are the standard choices.) It's even better if you make biscuits and break them up in the soup to thicken it.

 1 lb. boneless, skinless chicken thighs
 4 c. chicken broth
 2 (15 oz.) cans white beans, drained
 1½ tsp. salt
 ¼ tsp. pepper
 1 c. corn
 ½ onion, diced
 3 cloves minced garlic
 1 tsp. oregano
 1 tsp. chili powder
 1 tsp. ground cumin

Mash one can of white beans. Combine all ingredients except corn in a 3.5 quart slow cooker. Cook on high for 3-4 hours or on low for 6-8 hours. About 30 minutes before it's finished, stir in the corn and cover again.

Original Source: AmandasCookin.com (Crockpot White Chicken Chili)

Chicken Noodle Soup

 Cream of chicken soup (next recipe) OR 4 c. chicken broth
 1½ lb. chicken
 ¼ c. parsnips
 1 c. carrots
 ½ c. onions
 12 oz. egg noodles

Cook vegetables thoroughly, especially if they are a bit old. Heat the cream of chicken soup or chicken broth. Add remaining ingredients and simmer 10 minutes.

Original Source: MarthaStewart.com (Simple Chicken Noodle Soup)

SIMPLE COOKING FOR FAMILIES

Church Soup

As written this is admittedly bland, so you will probably want to add your own preferred herbs and spices, unless you use very flavorful bread. (Cornbread is great in this.)

> 1 onion, chopped
> ½ stick of butter
> 3 c. cooked navy beans OR 2 cans
> 4 c. milk

Combine in a large pot. Bring to the boiling point.

> Bread, cut into bite-sized pieces
> Salt and pepper to taste

Add.

Original Source: RecipeLion.com (Amish Church Soup)

Cream of Chicken or Turkey Soup

This is really just fancy, high calorie broth. It is definitely best viewed as the base for something else, in place of broth, unless you have someone sick who really can't eat much more than broth.

> ½ quart chicken or turkey broth
> ½ c. heavy cream OR ½ c. half and half
> ⅛ tsp. salt
> ⅛ tsp. pepper

Bring broth to a simmer. Slowly add cream, then seasoning. Cover and let rest on lowest for ten minutes. Serve hot or cold. This is really best served as the base for something else—add cooked meat, peas, carrots, or potatoes and whatever spices else you have on hand and might enjoy.

Original Source: theSpruceEats.com (Cream of Chicken or Turkey Soup)

Matzo Ball Soup

The original recipe called for 3-4 quarts of broth or salted water. The end result felt more like a broth than a soup because there was just sooo much liquid, and I'm reasonably sure it was a typo: they meant 3-4 CUPS of broth. With that said, I never had matzo ball soup before I made this. Now I'm definitely a fan!

> ¾ c. matzo meal
>
> ¼ tsp. garlic powder
>
> ¼ tsp. onion powder
>
> ¼ tsp. salt
>
> ¼ tsp. pepper
>
> 2 large eggs
>
> 2½ Tbsp. rendered chicken fat, grapeseed oil, or olive oil

Combine matzo meal, salt, garlic powder, onion powder, and pepper. In a second bowl, use another fork to mix the eggs and oil or rendered chicken fat (schmaltz). Pour into the dry ingredients. Don't overmix. Let rest in the refrigerator for 45 minutes.

> 4 c. broth OR salted water

While making 1" balls with the chilled matzo ball mixture, bring broth or salted water to a boil over medium heat. Matzo balls absorb some of what they are cooked in. If you cook them in broth instead of water, they will taste like chicken (or vegetables) and be more flavorful, but it can be made either way. Again, don't overwork the mixture. Lower temperature to a simmer and gently lower the matzo balls into it. Cook covered for 30 minutes, until thoroughly cooked.

For leftovers, remove the matzo balls and bring them to room temperature so they don't get mushy. If you will eat it soon, put both parts in the fridge in separate containers. If it will be more than a day or two, freeze it.

Original Source: ToriAvey.com (Sinker Matzo Balls)

Potato Soup

I love a nice, hearty bowl of potato soup on a cold day. I hadn't had any in years when I made this for the first time and it's even better than I remembered.

    5 slices bacon, diced

Add to a 4 quart pot, heated over medium-high heat, and cook until crispy. Move bacon to a plate. Keep 3 Tbsp. bacon grease in the pot, or use an equal amount of butter.

    1 c. onion
    1½ lb. potatoes, diced (Yukon gold recommended)

Dice onion and potatoes. Sauté onions 5 minutes, until soft. Set potatoes to the side until needed.

    4 cloves garlic

Add garlic and sauté an additional 1-2 minutes.

    ¼ c. flour
    2 c. chicken or vegetable stock

Add flour and sauté 1 minute, OR stir into stock. Add stock or mixture to sautéed items.

    2 c. milk, warmed

Add milk and potatoes. Cook until soup reaches a simmer. <u>Don't let it boil.</u> Reduce heat to medium-low. Cover. Simmer 10-15 minutes, stirring so the bottom doesn't burn. Potatoes should be soft. (Dicing them smaller makes this happen faster.)

    1 c. shredded cheddar cheese
    ½ c. Greek yogurt or sour cream
    1 tsp. salt
    ½ tsp. pepper

Stir in remaining ingredients. Season to taste.

Optional Toppings:

    Thin-sliced green onions or chives

133

Finely-shredded cheese

Extra bacon

Sour cream

Original Soursce: GimmeSomeOven.com (Potato Soup)

Pretzel Soup

This is a really odd soup, but when the cupboard is bare, it's bare. And this would be a good soup for anyone feeling sick.

Milk

Butter

Pretzels (soft pretzels, soda pretzels, or butter thin pretzels)

Heat a bowl of milk, leaving room to add pretzels. Add a small piece of butter (to taste). Break up or crush enough pieces of pretzel to fill the bowl. You can also use pieces of bread.

Original Source: AmishAmerica.com (Pretzel Soup)

Split Pea Soup

This takes a lot of time to make but very little effort. Most of the time is letting it simmer, unwatched. The actual prep time is negligible, and using a mandolin to slice the veggies made it even faster. This is also great with ham in it.

2 c. split peas, rinsed

6 c. cold water

Put the peas in the water and bring to a boil. Reduce heat and simmer for 1½ hour until split peas are tender. Drain.

1 carrot

1 celery stalk

1 onion

Chop carrot, celery, and onion.

5 c. chicken broth

3 garlic cloves

Optional Ingredients:

> 1 tsp. sugar
>
> 2 tsp. lemon juice
>
> 1 bay leaf
>
> Salt and pepper to taste
>
> Dash each of parsley, thyme, marjoram, and cayenne

Add all ingredients to the pot and return to a boil. Reduce heat and simmer for another 30 minutes, until carrots are tender. Remove the bay leaf. Cool slightly. Either puree in a blender or with a stick blender, or leave as is, depending on whether you prefer a smooth soup or not.

Original Source: CookingNook.com (Split Pea Soup)

12. Veggies/Side Dishes

We all know the drill: we need to eat veggies to be healthy. Veggies are also important to gut health and to proper intestinal function. In an emergency, a garden can provide fresh veggies when other food is scarce. Roasted vegetables are a quick, easy, healthy way to cook vegetables with little more than olive oil and a few herbs. Most of these recipes can easily be done using a variety of vegetables so experiment with your favorites until you find something you love.

Grains like quinoa and brown rice aren't as heavily processed as white rice. They need to be rinsed before cooking to remove some excess starch. Quinoa and brown rice are both great sides. A simple meal of poultry with a side of either of these makes a great meal. Add some veggies and you have a reasonably balanced meal.

Asparagus with Balsamic Butter Sauce

I have all the ingredients for this except butter in my long term storage.

> 1 bunch fresh asparagus, trimmed or 2 cans
> Salt and pepper to taste

Preheat oven to 400°F. Coat a cooking sheet with non-stick spray and arrange spears on it. Season with salt and pepper. Bake until tender, about 12 minutes. If you use canned and they are already tenderized (most are), reduce cook time to 5 minutes.

> 2 Tbsp. butter
>
> 2 Tbsp. soy sauce
>
> 1 tsp. balsamic vinegar

Melt butter over medium heat. Remove and add vinegar soy sauce. Pour over asparagus and serve.

Baked Potato (Sweet or White)

These are the basis for quite a few other foods. In an emergency, holding a fresh, hot baked potato is also a nice way to warm up a bit.

> Desired number of potatoes

Preheat oven to 350°F. Use a fork to make holes several places around the potatoes. If you prefer a crispy potato skin, coat them in olive oil or butter. Bake 50-60 minutes, until very soft. (Larger potatoes may require more baking time.) If you are in a hurry, cut potatoes in half and cook them on a baking sheet, skin side up for half the time, or stick a metal shishkabob skewer through the potato to help heat reach the center more quickly.

OR

Wrap each potato in cling wrap, being sure to cover the entire potato. Use a fork to make 6-10 holes around each potato. If you are out of cling wrap, remove a 1" deep sliver ⅛" wide running from one end to the other. Smaller spuds may be fully cooked in 5 minutes but larger ones should be flipped and cooked another five minutes.

Corn Fritters

> 1 c. flour
>
> 1 tsp. salt
>
> 1½ tsp. baking powder
>
> 1 tsp. pepper

Combine and mix well.

3 ears corn

1 egg

⅔ c. milk

Remove husks and silk from corn. Remove kernals. Lightly beat egg. Add corn kernals, egg, and milk to dry mix.

6 Tbsp. canola, grape seed, or sunflower oil

Put 2 Tbsp. oil in a frying pan over medium heat. When it's hot, add a heaping Tbsp. of batter. Press to flatten. Cook until golden (about 3 minutes), then flip and cook about 2 more minutes, until golden on both sides. Serve warm.

Cranberry Salad

I have always been horrible about eating my greens but I love this salad.

1 c. dried cranberries

½ c. walnuts

1 bag spinach

2 large oranges, peeled and seeded

2 apples, cored and chopped

2 Tbsp. honey

Chop all ingredients. Mix.

1 bottle raspberry vinaigrette (recipe page 72)

Top with vinaigrette and serve chilled.

Falafal

My goal is to provide variety and to look beyond what most people think about making in an emergency. In addition to the standard falafel balls, I shaped some into patties to make a falafel burger. Since I can't eat spices (including garlic), my falafel balls came out very dry but were still tasty with chutney and cheese.

16 oz. dried chickpeas, soaked, OR 4 cans (15 oz. each)

1 small onion

2 cloves garlic

Preheat oven to 400°F. Chop onions and garlic. Put in a food processor with chickpeas and chop finely. Don't turn it into mush.

½ bunch parsley

¼ bunch cilantro

1 Tbsp. cumin

¼ tsp. cayenne

Pepper to taste

1½ tsp. salt

Juice of ½ lemon (approximately 1 Tbsp.)

Add to mixture and pulse it until well incorporated but not mush. If you add all ingredients, it should be bright green.

¼ c. flour (chickpea works well)

2 Tbsp. tahini

Add to mixture. Pulse until well combined. Make 2 Tbsp. balls of the mixture. Bake 18 minutes. Flip and bake for 18 more minutes.

Original Source: FromMyBowl.com (Easy Falafal Recipe)

Four Bean Salad

Sometimes, it's the simple things in life, like this salad. I love how simple and easy to make it is! The fact that it uses nothing but long-term storage foods is just a bonus.

3 Tbsp. red wine vinegar

1 tsp. sugar

½ tsp. crushed red pepper

½ c. olive oil

Whisk together to make a dressing.

1 can (15.5 oz.) chick peas

1 can (15.5 oz.) black beans

1 can (15.5 oz.) cannellini

1 can (15.5 oz.) pinto beans

⅔ c. onion

½ c. tomato

2 Tbsp. cilantro

2 tsp. garlic

Drain beans. Combine all ingredients. Add dressing

French Fries (baked)

You can, of course, make any amount of French fries. This amount simply fills a cookie sheet nicely.

3 medium Russet potatoes

Cut to desired thickness. Put into a bowl, covered with cold water. Let stand in the refrigerator for one hour up to overnight. This helps remove some starch so the finished fries are crispy. When you remove the potatoes from the water, put them on a towel to remove extra moisture. Blot if needed.

1-2 Tbsp. olive oil

Put olive oil in a dry bowl with potatoes and any desired seasoning, such as sea salt. Combine. Bake spread out in one layer on a parchment-covered tray at 400°F for 15 minutes, flip and bake another 15 minutes. Finally, increase temperature to 425°F and bake 20 minutes. Fries should be golden brown and slightly crispy on the outside. Return to a bowl lined with towel if you aren't serving them immediately. If desired, sprinkle more salt, Parmesan cheese, or other seasoning on freshly baked fries.

Original Source: LayersofHappiness.com (Extra Crispy Baked French Fries)

Fried Rice

This is a great, flexible side. While these are the classic ingredients, you can switch them around based on what you have and like.

2 Tbsp. olive oil

1 small white onion

1 c. peas

3 eggs

3 cloves minced garlic

4 c. cooked rice, preferably day-old

2 medium carrots

2-3 Tbsp. soy sauce

2 Tbsp. green onions

Rice can be white or brown but should be chilled, not fresh. Whisk the eggs. Chop the onion and carrots into small pieces. If you use frozen peas and carrots, thaw them first. Pre-heat a wok or skillet to medium. Add olive oil. Fry onion, peas, and carrots until soft. Slide to the side. Cook eggs in the open space, scrambling with a spatula. When the eggs are cooked, mix in the vegetables and garlic. Cook one minute. Add rice and soy sauce. Mix well and heat thoroughly. Add chopped green onions to garnish.

Hummus, No Garlic

Hummus is incredibly simple to make, incredibly healthy, and incredibly easy to customize to your families taste. It even uses easily stored ingredients. What's not to love?

2 can (15 oz. each) chick peas

¼ c. + 2 Tbsp. reserved chick pea liquid

Drain beans and reserve the liquid.

¼ c. tahini

Juice of 1 lemon

1 tsp. salt

1 Tbsp. olive or sesame oil

Optional Ingredients:

Zest of 1 lemon

1 Tbsp. cumin

Pinch cayenne

Blend all ingredients except reserved liquid on low. Gradually add reserved liquid until desired consistency is achieved. Add optional toppings such as garlic, pine nuts, roasted red peppers, or chopped olives.

Mashed Maple Squash

Squash are great in emergencies because they stay good for a long time, especially stored somewhere cool and dark, like a cellar.

> 1 winter squash (acorn, butternut, etc.)
> 2 Tbsp. butter
> ¼ tsp. salt
> 2 Tbsp. maple syrup

Thoroughly cook and cool squash so you can handle it before starting the rest of the prep. Cut squash in half, remove all the seeds, and put the cut side down on a microwavable baking dish. Add ¼ c. water, cover with cling wrap, and microwave on high for 20 minutes. Once it's cool, scoop squash out of the skin, or just peel the skin and remove it.

Heat butter in a skillet. It is ready when it foams, starts smelling nutty, and browns a bit. Add squash and salt and continue cooking for 5-10 minutes. When that is done, stir in the maple syrup until well mixed. Serve warm.

Original Source: Cookistry.com (Blue Plate Special)

Mexicorn

This is sold canned, but it isn't complicated to make your own, and making your own allows you to change it up to suit your tastes. It's good added to grits, but it might be good in a quiche, omelette, or any number of other things.

> 1 red peppers
> 1 green peppers
> ½ red onion
> 4 oz. green chilies

Chop peppers, onions, and chilies into bite size pieces.

4 c. whole kernel corn

1½ Tbsp. butter

½ tsp. salt

Optional Ingredients:

1 Tbsp. chili powder

½ tsp. cilantro

Combine in a large saucepan over medium heat. Cover and cook 10-12 minutes.

Original Source: SixSistersStuff.com (Fresh Mexicorn)

Orange-Glazed Carrots

1 lb. baby carrots

Put carrots in a shallow sauce pan and cover with water. Boil until tender, about 10 minutes. Drain.

¼ c. orange juice

Pour orange juice over carrots and mix well. Simmer on medium heat about 5 minutes.

3 Tbsp. brown sugar

2 Tbsp. butter

1 pinch salt

Stir in remaining ingredients. Heat until butter and sugar melt.

Potato Croquettes

2 c. mashed potatoes

2 egg yolks

½ c. shredded Parmesan cheese

2 Tbsp. chives

1 Tbsp. flour

Chop the chives. Combine ingredients. Optional step: refrigerate for 30-60 minutes, until mixture is firm enough to not stick to your hands immediately. Roll into golf-ball size balls.

1-1 ½ c. vegetable or canola oil

Heat oil in a skillet over medium.

¾ c. bread crumbs

2 eggs

Put bread crumbs in a bowl. Beat eggs and put in a separate bowl. Dredge croquette balls in egg, then flour. Put croquettes in hot oil. Turn every minute or so to ensure even browning. After 3 minutes, they should be golden brown and done. Remove from heat and allow oil to drain off onto paper towels. Serve warm with sour cream or other sauce, if desired.

Original Source: PlatterTalk.com (Mashed Potato Croquette)

Poutine

I have heard of Poutine but never had it before sought out comfort food recipes for this book. My family's take on this is these are fancy French fries, but they are tasty. Add spices to taste.

WisconsinHomemaker.com suggests possibly using tater tots or sweet potato fries instead of regular French fries, and using feta cheese instead of cheese curds. I used broken up Mexican Queso Fresco from Walmart in place of cheese curds.

Gravy

3 Tbsp. cornstarch

2 Tbsp. water

In a small bowl, dissolve cornstarch in water. Set aside.

6 Tbsp. butter

¼ c. flour

Melt butter. Add flour. Cook 5 minutes, stirring regularly, until it turns golden brown.

20 oz. beef broth

10 oz. chicken broth

Pepper to taste

Add broth. Whisk. To thicken, add small amounts of cornstarch mix for about half, total. Add pepper to taste. Serve warm.

French Fries

>   2 lbs. Russet potatoes (3-4 medium)

Cut ½" thick sticks. Put into a bowl, covered with cold water. Let stand for one hour. When you remove the potatoes from the water and put on a paper towel, blot to remove extra moisture. Bake spread out on a parchment-covered tray at 425°F for 25 minutes. Start cooking them but stop before they begin to brown. Return to a bowl lined with towel, if you aren't serving them immediately.

>   1-1½ c. white cheese curds OR Queso Fresco

To serve, put warm fries in a bowl and season with salt. Add gravy and toss fries so they are all coated. Add cheese curds and toss again. Add freshly ground pepper.

Original Source: SeasonsandSuppers.ca (Authentic Canadian Poutine)

Quinoa

I hesitated to try making quinoa because I had no idea what it was or how to cook it. Quinoa is actually as easy as rice, and people have successfully made rice for thousands of years, long before timers or electric ovens. Quinoa comes in white, red, and black varieties, with white recommended as the one to try first. You might experiment with substituting it for rice in fried rice and other meals.

>   1 c. quinoa
>   1¾ c. water or broth
>   1 tsp. olive oil

Before cooking quinoa, rinse it thoroughly by swishing under cool running water in a mesh strainer. This removes a natural coating that can make it taste slightly soapy or bitter.

Heat olive oil over medium heat in a small saucepan. When it is shimmering, add drained quinoa. Cook 2 minutes, stirring constantly, until the water evaporates and quinoa is toasted. Add the liquid (water or broth) and bring to a rolling boil. Reduce heat to lowest setting and cover. Cook 15 minutes. Remove from heat and let stand 5 minutes before removing the cover. If any liquid remains at the bottom, return to low heat and cook (covered) for another 5 minutes. Fluff and eat.

Rice, Brown

> 1 c. brown rice
> 6 c. cold water
> 1½ tsp. salt

Rinse rice in cold water for 30 seconds. Boil water and salt. Add rice and cook on medium-high for thirty minutes, stirring occasionally. Don't cover the pot completely or it will boil over, but do cover it most of the way. When it finishes boiling, drain water off but keep rice in the pot. Cover tightly and let set for twenty minutes while steam finishes cooking the rice. Uncover, fluff, and eat.

Rice, White

Rice really is as simple as this recipe. Double, triple, or quadruple this recipe, based on your family needs. You can also replace the water with whey, a by-product of making cheese, to add a slightly different flavor.

> 1 c. white rice
> 2 c. water

Boil water. Add rice. Simmer covered on low for 20 minutes. Remove from heat. Eat.

My mother in law was adamant that the crispy rice on the bottom of the pan is a treat, especially for kids.

Roasted Squash and Apples

With some protein (chicken), this could be a lovely main dish.

> 1½ lbs. acorn squash
> 2 apples

Preheat oven to 425°F. Cut squash in half and remove the seeds. Peel and core apples. Cut both into 1" wedges.

>   3 Tbsp. olive oil
>   ½ tsp. salt
>   ½ tsp. pepper
>   ¾ tsp. cinnamon
>   ½ tsp. allspice
>   ½ tsp. coriander

Combine spices and whisk together with oil. Coat squash and apples. Combine all ingredients and put on greased rimmed baking pan or in a casserole dish. Roast 25-30 minutes. Apples and squash are ready to eat when tender.

>   ¼ c. dried cherries

Top with dried cherries.

Original Source: Eating Well, September/October 2018 (Roasted Squash & Apples with Dried Cherries & Pepitas)

Twice-Baked Potatoes

>   4 medium potatoes

Preheat oven to 400°F. Poke holes in potato that is scrubbed clean and bake until tender, 45-60 minutes. To bake in a microwave, wrap the potato in cling wrap, poke 4-6 holes in it and bake for 5 minutes. Cool for 10 minutes.

Cut a slice from the top of the potato, enough to allow you to scoop out the pulp, leaving ¼" thickness on the outside. Return shells to oven for 10 minutes to make them crispy.

>   1 c. grated cheese
>   ¼ c. sour cream or Greek yogurt
>   ¼ c. buttermilk
>   4 Tbsp. butter
>   2 strips bacon (baked)

Mix pulp and remaining ingredients with fork and stuff the potato with it. Return potato to the oven and broil for 5-10 minutes, or 2-3 minutes in the microwave, until thoroughly cooked.

Original Source: TheCookieRookie.com (Best Twice Baked Potatoes)

13. Sushi

Sushi isn't an obvious thing to include in an emergency preparedness cookbook since it's most famous for having raw fish, but sushi can actually contain vegetables only and all kinds of other things. The basic sushi recipe is two kinds of vegetables plus one source of fish. Both nori (seaweed) and brown rice are actually quite healthy, and white rice isn't all that bad either, so it's really about finding fillings that work for your family.

There are a few reasons I like sushi for emergency preparedness. It is a way to use small amounts of leftovers. The basic ingredients–rice and dried seaweed–don't need refrigerated and won't go bad quickly. (Sushi does typically have some oil so it has a somewhat limited shelf-life, similar to nuts or brown rice.) It's easy to let each person customize their sushi. It doesn't need a lot of fancy equipment. And it's easy to carry, especially if you learn to make hand rolls.

You can technically wrap just about any food with rice and seaweed and make sushi, not just fish. There are two ingredients you simply must have to make sushi: seaweed (nori) and rice. "Sushi rice" is preferable because its stickiness helps everything hold together, but it isn't a deal breaker. (Sushi rice is a specific kind of rice just like brown rice and long grain rice.) Take any food you enjoy, use the "basic sushi" recipe, and you can have sushi. Modify the recipes here until you have ones you like. That's basically what I did to create these recipes, all of which use fully cooked ingredients, although raw are most commonly used. Personally, I find myself adding cream cheese to most sushi rolls simply because I like the texture. There is a ton of information online about making sushi. "MakeSushi.com" is a great place to learning about making sushi and it's a great place for inspiration. Mix and match to create your own favorites!

NOTE: Full cooking/assembly instructions are only given for the first recipe, "basic sushi". Refer to this until you are comfortable with the technique. The remaining recipes focus on the filling.

Sushi Rice

> 1 c. sushi rice (a.k.a., sweet rice or glutinous rice)
>
> 1 Tbsp. vinegar, preferably rice wine
>
> 3 c. water

Rinse rice repeatedly until the water remains clear. Boil water. Add rice and simmer uncovered for 10 minutes. Cover and simmer 10 more minutes or until all water has been absorbed. Remove from heat and cool 10 minutes. Move rice to a bowl that isn't metal and add rice wine vinegar a little at a time. (Metal bowls may react to vinegar, giving the rice a slight metallic taste.) The vinegar helps keep the grains of rice more separate, less mushy, and helps keep bacteria from growing and multiplying.

Not-Sushi-Rice for Sushi

> 1½ c. short-grain rice or 1 c. long-grain rice
>
> 2 c. water (optional: add 2 Tbsp. extra water for stickiness)

Soak rice for 30 minutes to 4 hours. Boil water. Add rice and simmer uncovered for 10 minutes. Cover and simmer 10 more minutes or until all water has been absorbed. Remove from heat and allow to cool for at least 10 minutes.

Making Not-Sushi-Rice Stickier

Rice needs to be at least moderately sticky to help sushi rolls stay together. Sushi rice is naturally this way but other kinds of rice need all the help they can get to make them stickier.

- Short-grain rice tends to have more starch, and therefore be stickier, than medium- or long-grain rice. Jasmine and basmati are both medium-grain rice, and popular in the US.
- Unlike sushi rice, don't rinse other kinds of rice repeatedly before cooking.
- Leaving non-sushi rice soak in water for 30 minutes to 4 hours before cooking may help make it be stickier.
- Letting cooked rice set in the pot longer can help it get stickier.

Basic Sushi Preparation

This is a short, probably over-simplified version of how to make sushi. Search online for videos if you need help. As you make more, you will learn your family's preferences. As I made more sushi, I found myself decreasing the rice, down to ¼ c. of rice per roll.

1 c. rice

1 sheet of nori (seaweed)

¾ c. filling

Put a sheet of nori shiny side down on the sushi mat*. Spread rice in a thin layer from the top of the nori to the bottom and left to right, **leaving 2.5" on one side without rice**. Put filling in a line from the top to bottom near the edge with rice. You can put condiments such as wasabi in with the filling, or sprinkle in some spices.

> *Rolling sushi is easiest with a sushi mat. They are inexpensive and widely available, including online and in gift sets. You can even use a kitchen tea towel or a thick paper towel.

Moisten the end with exposed nori just enough so to be sticky. The ends are normally dampened with rice vinegar but water can be used, too. Fold the end near the filling over the filling, then roll the whole thing up tightly until only the edge with exposed nori is left, being sure to press the filling into the rice as you roll it, but not so much that you squeeze all the filling out the ends. Roll over the dampened nori and hold it there for a little while so it will seal closed. Cut your sushi into pieces with a very sharp knife and serve. Make additional rolls if filling ingredients allow. Roll, cut, and eat.

Chicken Tempura Sushi

> 1 c. rice
>
> 1 sheet of nori (seaweed)
>
> ½ c. chicken tempura*
>
> 2 oz. cream cheese from a block (not tub)
>
> *Tempura is a Japanese style of battering and frying.

Cut chicken into strips and cook following vegetable tempura recipe. Spread rice on the nori. Make a line down the nori with chicken, then slices of cream cheese. Roll, cut, eat.

Omelet Sushi

If desired, you can include meat, veggies, cheese, etc. in the omelet.

> 1 c. rice
>
> 1 sheet of nori (seaweed)
>
> 1 egg omelet

Spread rice on the nori. Slice omelet into strips. Put omelet strips in a strip down the omelet. Roll, cut, and eat.

Orange-Glazed Sushi

> 1 c. rice
>
> 1 sheet of nori (seaweed)
>
> 2 oz. cream cheese from a block (not tub)
>
> 1 full carrot
>
> ½ c. baked chicken breast

Spread rice on the nori. Cut chicken into strips length-wise. Cook carrot following the Orange Glazed Carrots recipe, cutting carrots into strips and adding chicken with the last ingredients. Put pieces of each in a line from the top of the nori to the bottom starting about ¾ of the way down and add cream cheese beside it. Roll, cut, and eat.

Philadelphia(ish) Sushi

    1 c. rice
    1 sheet of nori (seaweed)
    1 c. mixed roasted vegetables
    ¼ c. cream cheese from a block (not tub)

Spread rice on the nori. Put cream cheese and vegetables in a line down the nori. Roll, cut, and eat.

Roast Vegetable Sushi

    1 c. rice
    1 sheet of nori (seaweed)
    ¾ c. mixed vegetables

Spread rice on the nori. Put veggies in a line down the nori. Roll, cut, and eat.

Rosemary Chicken Sushi

    1 c. rice
    1 sheet of nori (seaweed)
    ½ c. baked chicken with rosemary
    ¼ c. roasted veggies

Spread rice on the nori. Make a line down the nori with chicken, then with veggies. Roll, cut, eat.

Shepherd's Pie Sushi

    1 c. mashed potato
    1 sheet of nori (seaweed)
    ¼ c. green beans, fully cooked
    ½ c. lamb or chicken

1 carrot, fully cooked

Spread mashed potato on the nori. If desired, add any spice or herb you enjoy to the vegetables and/or lamb. Slice carrots and meat lengthwise. Put green beans, carrots, and lamb in a line from the top to the bottom of the nori. Roll and refrigerate. Cut and eat cool so mashed potatoes are firm.

Shrimp Tempura Sushi

1 c. rice

1 sheet of nori (seaweed)

1-2 shrimp tempura

Make shrimp tempura. Spread rice on the nori. Make a line down the nori with shrimp. Add veggies in a line, if desired. Roll, cut, eat.

Thanksgiving Sushi

1 c. baked sweet or white potato

1 sheet of nori (seaweed)

½ c. baked turkey

2 Tbsp. cranberry sauce

Spread mashed sweet or white potatoes on the nori. Slice the turkey into strips length-wise. Spoon the cranberry sauce out in a line from the top of the sheet to the bottom. Finish by adding pieces of turkey, then roll, cut, and eat.

14. Main Dishes

I grew up eating a lot of casseroles. I think that was part of the 1970s, but it was also part of having a working mom and not having a grocery store of any kind around the corner. Casseroles are quick, easy, often rely on canned goods, and are forgiving of substitutions if you run out of something else. A good stir-fry or pasta dish is similarly forgiving, making them good emergency (and family) meals. Boxed (dried) pasta has the additional benefit of being a good long-term storage food, if you don't make homemade.

This just may be the most eclectic chapter in this book, which is saying something. I'll be honest, I can't think of a way shrimp tempura counts as an emergency meal, but homemade is *so much* cheaper than store-bought and my kids just love it, so it's in here.

Brown Sugar Chops

I love the simplicity of this recipe.

> 6 pork chops
> 6 Tbsp. brown sugar
> 6 Tbsp. butter
> 1 Tbsp. soy sauce

Preheat oven to 350°F. Put chops in 9x13" casserole dish. Top each one with 1 Tbsp. each of brown sugar and butter. Sprinkle with soy sauce. Cover pan with foil and bake for 45 minutes. Remove foil. Bake 15 more minutes, until browned.

CCC Casserole

This is a Scout recipe. It is designed to be cooked on a campfire. Cooking it in an oven is the modified recipe. You can substitute canned meat for fresh.

> ½ lb. ground chicken, turkey, or lamb
> 1½ c. crushed corn chips
> 1 can chili (or equivalent in homemade chili)
> 1 c. cheese, grated

Brown the ground meat. Drain excess grease and add chili. Mix and stir until it reaches a boil, then simmer for about five minutes. Put the corn chips in the bottom of a 9x9 baking dish. Add the meat and chili mix, then top with cheese. Cover and bake at 350°F for 20 minutes.

Original Source: Boy Scout Campouts

Chicken Nuggets

There doesn't seem to be any getting around it: kids like nuggets. A desire to cook your own food, be self-sufficient, eat healthier, etc. doesn't change that. This recipe is easy to make and healthier, at least.

> ½ c. olive oil
> 4 cloves garlic, minced
> ¼ tsp. pepper
> 1 lb. chicken

Mix olive oil, garlic, and pepper to make a marinade. Cut chicken into nugget size pieces. Put chicken in a bowl and cover with marinade or toss it in the bowl with the marinade, being sure to fully coat all chicken. Marinate for 30 minutes in the refrigerator.

> ½ c. flour, corn meal, or panko

¼ tsp. ginger

¼ tsp. pepper

¼ tsp. salt

Preheat oven to 475°F. Combine flour and spices in a bowl. Remove chicken from marinade and dredge in mixture to completely coat it. Bake 15 minutes and flip. Cook 10 more minutes, until both sides are brown.

Original Source: The Healthy Gut Cookbook

Couscous with Dried Cherries

This is one of my favorite lunches because it's so fast and easy to make. Added bonus: leftovers heat up quickly, too.

1 c. chicken broth

¼ c. water

2 oz. dried sour cherries

1 Tbsp. butter

1 pinch salt

Pepper to taste

Combine ingredients in a medium saucepan. Bring to a boil over medium to medium-high heat. If you use bouillon, add an extra ¼ c. water because some of it will have evaporated while reaching boiling.

1 c. couscous, pastini, or other small dried pasta

Add couscous. Cover, remove from heat, and let stand 5 minutes. Fluff with a fork and serve. If desired, add chunks of chicken, additional vegetables, or spices for variety.

Cuban Potato Balls

This is probably the most complex recipe in this cookbook, but they are just so darn tasty! This is a long recipe but basically you make mashed potatoes, then a beef filling. You wrap the beef in mashed potatoes, bread it, and cook it. The original recipe calls for frying, but I prefer baking. I use more mashed potatoes than the recipe calls for because I have a hard time getting the potato layer thin enough, andI really like mashed potatoes.

It's hard to know exactly how much potatoes you will need because how thick you make the outside potato or how much filling you put in can change the ratio drastically. Any leftover stuffing makes a good burrito filling, among other things. And leftover burrito filling can make a good potato ball filling.

> 4 large potatoes, peeled and cubed (approximately 5 c. mashed potatoes)
>
> 1 Tbsp. warm milk
>
> ½ tsp. salt

Peel and cube potatoes, then boil until soft, about 20-25 minutes. Pierce with a fork to confirm they are soft all the way through, but not mushy. Mash with milk, salt, and butter. You can use an equal amount of boxed mashed potatoes. Line a tray with a silicone mat or parchment paper. Press mashed potatoes into a layer on the pan. The dough should be just thick enough that the stuffing won't peak through. Refrigerate for 30 minutes or until the dough doesn't stick when you handle it.

> 2 small green bell peppers (about 1 c.)
>
> 2 small red bell peppers (about 1 c.)
>
> 1 onion
>
> 2 garlic cloves

Finely chop onion and peppers. Peel and chop garlic.

> 1 Tbsp. vegetable oil
>
> 1 lb. ground sirloin

Heat a large pot over medium high heat. Drizzle in the vegetable oil and add sirloin. Break up the beef to help it cook and brown. Once it has browned, add the onion and garlic. Stir until the onions are translucent. Add finely chopped peppers.

> 1 lime (approximately 2 Tbsp.)
>
> ½ tsp. salt

1 tsp. black pepper

1 tsp. paprika

1 tsp. cumin

1 tsp. dried oregano

1 Tbsp. Worchestershire

Juice lime. Add seasonings including lime juice to pot. Pull the potatoes out of the refrigerator. Cut circles in the mashed potatoes.* Put a scoop of filling in the center of each potato circle. Bring sides together to make a ball around the filling. Continue until you run out of dough and/or filling. Reshape leftover bits to make more circles.

2 eggs

1 Tbsp. water

Whisk eggs and water together in a dish.

1 c. bread crumb

¼ c. flour

Preheat oven to 350°F. Combine bread crumbs and flour in a second dish. Dip each ball into the egg mixture, then the flour mixture to lightly cover, placing them on parchment lined baking sheets. Cook 10 minutes then flip and cook an additional 10 minutes. You can freeze uncooked potato balls for another day.

Deep Dish Pizza (NOT Chicago style)

This dough can make two 8" pizza crusts. It can also be used to make bread or breadsticks.

2½ c. medium hot water

5 tsp. instant yeast OR 2 Tbsp. regular yeast

Pour water in a mixing bowl and sprinkle with yeast. Don't stir. Allow yeast to dissolve. This can take 30 minutes or more. The more evenly spread the yeast is and the larger the surface is it on (wide flat bowl versus taller thinner one), the faster it will dissolve.

2 Tbsp. sugar

3 Tbsp. oil

1 tsp. salt

6 c. whole wheat or all-purpose flour*

4 Tbsp. butter

*A combination of whole wheat and all-purpose works too.

Add sugar, salt, and oil after the yeast has dissolved. Combine. Gradually add flour. Preheat oven to 400°F. Put butter in a cake pan (or whatever you use to bake the pizza) in the preheating oven 2-3 minutes, until butter is melted. Divide dough in half and form into two balls. Flatten one ball and press onto pan, letting butter get on top of the dough. To finish, add sauce, cheese, and toppings to taste. Cook 10-12 minutes or until cheese is slightly browned. Crust will rise and become firm.

Fettucine Alfredo

The original recipe assume you are using fresh pasta. If you are, that's great! You don't need cook the pasta until the sauce is simmering. For the rest of us, it's better to start the pasta closer to the same time we start the sauce, based on what the package instructions say.

1 pkg. (12 oz.) fettucine

Cook pasta.

1½ Tbsp. butter

Melt in a saucepan over medium heat.

1 Tbsp. flour

Add to flour and stir until golden brown.

1½ c. milk

Add and whisk until sauce thickens, about 5 minutes. Whisking helps prevent lumps.

2 Tbsp. Neufchatel (low-cal cream cheese)

½ c. grated Parmesan

1 tsp. grated lemon zest

Salt to taste

Stir in. Reduce to a simmer to keep warm. If you are using fresh pasta, cook it now. Drain pasta and add it to the sauce. Combine to ensure all pasta is well coasted and serve. Top with more grated Parmesan, if desired.

Original Source: EatThis.com (Healthy Fettucine Alfredo)

Foil Dinner

This is another Scout campfire classic, but does well in the oven.

> 1 lb. potatoes
> 1 red bell pepper
> 1 onion
> ½ tsp. vegetable oil
> 1 lb. chorizo, casing removed

Heat grill or oven to 400°F. Slice everything into bite-size pieces. Oil 6 sheets of aluminum foil and put 1½-2 c. of mixture on each. Fold foil over mixture and seal closed. Cook 25-30 minutes, turning halfway through. Open carefully and add seasoning, to taste.

(Oven) Fried Chicken

This is basic comfort food, but it's also a good start for sandwiches, salads, and more. As a note, the original recipe said ¼ CUP salt, but I just can't believe that. ¼ tsp. works just fine.

> 8 chicken drumsticks
> 4 c. non-fat buttermilk
> ¼ tsp. salt
> ¼ c. sugar

Combine. Refrigerate 2-12 hours.

> 1 Tbsp. hot sauce
> 2 c. panko bread crumbs
> 2 Tbsp. canola or vegetable oil
> 1 tsp. chili powder
> ½ tsp. garlic salt

Preheat oven to 350°F and line a rimmed baking sheet with parchment paper. Combine ingredients. Break lumps apart. Remove one drumstick at a time from marinade, allowing extra liquid to drip off. Toss in breadcrumbs and thoroughly coat. Put drumsticks on baking sheet. Bake on the middle rack for 15 minutes. Flip and bake another 15 minutes. When finished, panko will be evenly browned and chicken will be cooked through.

Original Source: EatThis.com (Oven Fried Chicken)

Gyoza

Gyoza needs some vegetables in the filling. Swap out anything you don't have for something you do. It's very flexible.

> 1 pkg. gyoza wrappers (no need to thaw them)
> ½ lb. chicken or turkey*
> 1 can (9 oz.) water chestnuts
> 1 Tbsp. olive oil
> 1 tsp. ginger powder
> Vegetables to taste
> 1 c. carrots
> 1c. peppers
> ¼ c. mushrooms
> *Leftover taco meat makes a great start to gyoza filling.

Grate carrots. Mince the other solid ingredients into small pieces. Mix everything together. Gyoza wrappers can be frozen when you start filling them. Use your finger to moisten one edge of the wrapper so it stays shut when crimped. Spoon 1 Tbsp. filling into the center of each wrapper, fold wrapper in half, and crimp the edges shut so nothing falls out. Continue until you are out of wrappers or filling.

Put finished gyoza in a non-stick or greased skillet or wok over medium heat with 2 Tbsp. of water. Cover and steam for 5 minutes. Remove lid and continue cooking for 5 minutes, then flip them. Cook 5 more minutes. Check to be sure they are fully cooked before serving.

If not, flip and cook 5 more minutes. You can freeze leftovers to eat later.

You can also fry gyoza.

Gyoza sauce is half vinegar and half soy sauce, mixed.

Ham and Cheese Croquettes

I used pieces of sliced sandwich turkey instead of ham because of my allergy issues and my husband's comment was, "This would be really good with ham." So there you go!

> 2 Tbsp. butter
> 1 Tbsp. olive oil
> ¼ c. white onion
> Salt and pepper to taste

Finely chop onion. Heat butter and oil over medium. After butter melts, add onion, salt and pepper. Cook until onion is translucent.

> ⅓ c. + 1 Tbsp. flour

Add flour slowly to reduce clumping. Cook 1 minute

> ¾ c. milk

Whisk in slowly until flour is no longer clumpy. Cook 3 minutes, continuing to whisk. It should thicken.

> ⅓ c. ham
> ⅓ c. finely grated cheese

Finely chop ham. Add ham and cheese to mixture. Cool in refrigerator. When you can handle, scoop tablespoons of mixture and form into ovals.

> 2 eggs
> ¼ c. panko
> ¼ c. breadcrumbs
> ¼ c. finely grated cheese

Whisk eggs. Combine panko, breadcrumbs, and cheese in another bowl. Roll croquettes in breadcrumbs, then egg, then in breadcrumbs a second time.

Vegetable oil

Heat 2-3" of vegetable oil to 375°F. Carefully lower 3-4 croquettes at a time into the oil. Cook for 1-2 minutes. Remove from oil with a slotted spoon when golden brown and put on a paper towel to absorb oil.

Original Source: TheKittchen.com (Ham and Cheese Croquette)

Macaroni and Cheese

It's a well-loved comfort food, but this version is healthy. You can't even taste the squash.

> 3 c. dry pasta
> 1 Tbsp. olive oil
> ½ c. roughly chopped white onion
> 2 cloves garlic, minced
> 1½ c. vegetable broth
> 3 c. diced butternut squash, about ¾ of a medium squash
> ¼ tsp. each salt and pepper

Prepare pasta according to instructions on the box. While it boils, put olive oil in a large pot over medium heat with the onion and garlic. Cook thoroughly, about 5 minutes. Add the broth, butternut, and spices and simmer for 7-10 minutes, until butternut is thoroughly cooked. Puree the mixture until smooth.

> 1 c. shredded mild cheddar cheese
> ½ c. plain Greek yogurt

Strain the pasta and add the puree, then the cheddar cheese. When that is well mixed, add the yogurt and stir until well mixed.

Original Source: AmandasCookin.com (Butternut Squash Mac and Cheese)

Manicotti Stuffed with Goat Cheese

8 manicotti shells

¼ tsp. pepper

½ tsp. olive oil

1 clove minced garlic

1¼ c. cottage cheese

3 oz. goat cheese

Make shells and set aside. Preheat oven to 400°F. If desired, cook garlic for 30 seconds. Mix all ingredients except the shells. Fill each shell with 3 Tbsp. of cheese mixture and place in a shallow baking dish. Top with a sauce such as the roasted red pepper sauce or canned pasta sauce. Bake 25 minutes or until the sauce bubbles.

Meatballs

This is another great way to help your meat go farther, and an excellent place to use some TVP.

1 lb. ground chicken or turkey (raw)

1 egg, beaten

¼ c. bread crumbs

¼ c. grated parmesan cheese

¼ c. onion

2 tsp. minced garlic

¾ tsp. kosher salt

¼ tsp. pepper

2 Tbsp. parsley

Preheat oven to 400°F. Combine all ingredients. If needed, add 1-2 Tbsp. water at a time to keep the mixture wet. Form into 1½" balls. (A cookie scoop works well.) Place on a baking sheet lined with parchment paper. Bake 8-10 minutes, uncovered, then flip and bake for another 8-10 minutes.

Original Source: IHeartNaptime.ne (Meatball Recipe)

Pierogi

Pierogi is actually the plural for the much-less-used peirog. Now that's a thing you know.

>3 c. flour
>Pinch kosher salt

Pour flour onto a counter or other clean work surface. Add salt. Make a hole in the middle of the flour. It should look like a volcano.

>½ c. warm milk
>1 Tbsp. melted unsalted butter

Mixing as you go, gradually pour milk and butter into the hole in the center of the flour.

>½-¾ c. warm water

Add a little at a time. You need to be able to form a ball. Cover mixed dough with a larger bowl. Let rest for 20-30 minutes and start filling.

>5 medium yellow or 3 large russet potatoes

Skin potatoes and cut into chunks. Put chunks in a pot. Cover with water and cook over medium heat until tender.

>1 onion
>1 Tbsp. oil or ghee

Heat oil/ghee in a frying pan. Cook onions to golden brown.

>8 oz. farmer cheese*
>1 Tbsp. Blue cheese (optional)
>2 Tbsp. Cheddar cheese (optional)
>½ tsp. garlic powder
>½ tsp. onion powder
>Kosher salt and freshly ground pepper to taste
>*There are different substitutes recommended online, but I
>   just used Mexican Queso Fresco from Walmart.

Mash fork-tender potatoes until they don't have lumps. Add onions, cheeses, and spices. Combine thoroughly and set aside.

Roll out the dough out like pasta (thin). I recommend using a pasta maker to do this; doing it by hand is extremely hard. Cut out circles. Put 1 tsp. of filling in the center. Wet half of the circle with your finger, then fold dough over the center and press it closed. Repeat with remaining circles.

To Boil: Boil a pot of salted water. Boil 8 at a time. Once they float to the top, cook each pierogi 1 more minute before removing with a slotted spoon.

To Fry: Put 1 Tbsp. oil or ghee in a pan over medium heat. Fry pierogis until golden brown on each side.

Original Source: EatingEuropoean.com (Authentic Polish Pierogi)

Pizza Bagels

In college, I had a pizza bagel for lunch or dinner almost every day for an entire year. Today, my kids love mini pizza bagels but I don't love buying them frozen ones all the time. This is my solution.

> 6 bagels or 12 mini bagels
> 1 can pizza or tomato sauce
> Cheese
> Toppings

Preheat the oven to 450°F. Slice bagels in half. Put approximately 2 Tbsp. of sauce on each bagel half, 1 Tbsp. for a mini-bagel. Add cheese and toppings to taste. Bake for 11 minutes.

Pulled Chicken

Despite my initial fears, making this pulled chicken was quick, easy, and tasty. I used it for sliders and in sushi. It is one of the most surprising successes I've had in writing this cookbook.

> 4 boneless skinless chicken breasts cut into thirds
> 1 Tbsp. apple cider vinegar with the mother

2 Tbsp. brown sugar

1⅓ c. barbeque or other sauce, divided

¼ c. water

Use a liner for your slow cooker. Reserve half (⅔ c.) of sauce for later. Add all the other ingredients to slow cooker. Cover and cook on low for five hours or on high for 2½ to 3 hours. Remove chicken with a straining spoon. Shred chicken with two forks. Return chicken to the pot and mix into the cooking liquid. Stir in remaining sauce and enjoy.

Shake and Bake Chicken

My tween pronounced this "better than other chicken you made", which I count as a resounding endorsement. My husband and I both like it a lot, so it has gone into fairly regular rotation in our house.

Shake and bake mix

Chicken or other protein

Dump enough of mix to coat all the protein into a gallon zippered plastic bag. Rinse chicken or other protein. When excess water is gone, put it in the bag, seal it, then shake to coat. Remove and put on a lined cookie sheet. Bake at 425°F for 15-20 minutes.

Original Source: TheBlackPeppercorn.com (Homemade Shake n Bake)

Shepherd's Pie

I remember this from my childhood. There are many things that were popular in the 60s and 70s that I'm happy to see consigned to the dustbin of history, but this is one I'd be happy to see come back.

3 medium white or sweet potatoes

Peel and quarter the potatoes. Put them in a pot and cover with at least an inch of cold water and bring to a boil. Reduce and simmer until tender, about 20 minutes.

½ stick butter

1 c. each of 2-3 mixed vegetables (diced carrots, corn, peas, green beans, peppers, etc.)

While potatoes cook, melt butter in a skillet over medium heat and sauté vegetables, starting with carrots because they take longer. Peas and corn cook quickly so put them in last. You can use as little as 1 c. of one vegetable, but it tastes better with 3-4 c. mixed veggies.

2 lbs. ground lamb

½ c. broth

Salt, pepper, and spices to taste

When vegetables are ready, add lamb and finish cooking mixture. Add salt, pepper, and broth. When broth starts simmering, reduce heat to low and cook uncovered for 10 minutes. If lamb starts drying out, add more broth.

Preheat oven to 400°F. Mash the potatoes. Spread the lamb and vegetable mixture evenly in the bottom of a 9x9 casserole dish. Layer the mashed potatoes over the lamb/vegetable mixture. Cook about thirty minutes, until browned and bubbling.

Original Source: SimplyRecipes.com (Easy Shepherd's Pie)

Shishkabobs

Skewers

1 lb. protein or meatballs

½ lb. potatoes or sweet potatoes

½ lb. veggies such as bell peppers or onions

½ c. sauce

Cut all ingredients into bite-size pieces. Alternate ingredients on skewers. Brush with sauce. Cook over medium heat until thoroughly cooked, 6-8 minutes. Use any available vegetables.

Ham and pineapple with sweet and sour sauce is a classic combination.

Shrimp Tempura

My family loves shrimp tempura, but I don't love the cost. This is far more budget-friendly. I highly recommend JustOneCookbook.com's very helpful post "How to Prepare Shrimp to Shrimp Tempura & Ebi Fry." This makes A LOT of tempura batter, so you might want to cut it in half and drink half the can of soda.

　　1 lb. shrimp, veined

If frozen, thaw overnight. Remove shells from the body of the shrimp, leaving the tails on. Lay them on a cutting board, bottom-side up. Make 3 small cuts on the bottom so shrimp lays flat. Rinse shrimp. Make a small cut in the center of the tail to prevent splatter as liquid in there heats. (Read the post mentioned above for a more thorough explanation.)

　　1½ c. tempura (or flour – rice, all-purpose, wheat, any kind)
　　½ tsp. salt
　　1 12 oz. can seltzer water or club soda, chilled
　　1-1½ c. canola oil

Whisk flour, salt, and seltzer together. Pour half a cup of oil into a non-stick or cast iron skillet over medium-high heat. While the oil heats, coat shrimp lightly in batter. You can hand-dip them or toss them using a flat whisk, which also allows extra batter to drain off. (I used a dipping fork designed for coating things with chocolate.) Put shrimp in hot oil until crispy and very lightly browned on the bottom (2-3 minutes), then flip and cook another 2-3 minutes, being sure the shrimp are fully cooked. Don't crowd the pan. Remove and put on a paper towel to drain excess oil.

Before putting in the next batch, check oil and add up to an additional half cup. Allow oil to heat up to around 360°F again so they stay crispy and tasty.

Seasoning options:

Add 1-2 Tbsp. of your preferred spices to the batter, as long as they are light enough to stay suspended in batter and cooking oil.

Stuffed Acorn Squash

This is easy to carry along and eat later, whether that's at lunch at work or hiking in the woods, although time becomes an issue if it isn't refrigerated because it contain meat.

> 4 c. cooked brown rice
>
> 2 medium acorn squash, seeded
>
> 1 lb. ground chicken, turkey, or lamb
>
> ½ c. chopped, peeled apple
>
> ½ c. shredded cheese

Brown the meat. Add the apples. Microwave squash for five minutes, then cut in half from top to bottom. Combine the rice, meat, and apples, and stuff the squash with it. Cover with cling wrap and microwave until the squash is cooked through and soft, about five minutes. Top with the cheese and microwave 1 more minute.

Teriyaki Burger

The first time I made these, I didn't realize the second pound of ground beef had gone bad until after I dumped the first pound in. That made the mixture too soft for a burger, but it made a good Manwich-type sandwich, and a good filling for Cuban Potato Balls.

> 1 egg
>
> ½ c. teriyaki sauce
>
> ½ c. saltines

Lightly beat egg. Crush saltines with a mortar and pestle. Combine ingredients.

> 2 lbs. ground beef or turkey

Add to mixture. Divide into 8 parts. Form each part into a ball, then smash into patties. Take out wax or parchment paper. Stack burgers, separated by wax or parchment paper, and marinate in refrigerator for a few hours or overnight.

> 20 oz. pineapple slices (fresh or canned)
>
> 8 hamburger buns

Grill burgers for 6 minutes per side, until done. At the same time, lightly grill pineapple slices. If you like grilled buns, grill them until toasty. Add desired toppings and enjoy!

Original Source: TheFrugalGirls.com (Easy Teriyaki Burger)

Teriyaki Wings

Wings don't normally have a place in emergency preparedness cookbooks, but wings make people happy. Plus, if you have a whole chicken, you'll need to do something with the wings.

> 12 chicken wings
>
> ¼ c. vegetable oil
>
> ½ c. teriyaki sauce

Preheat oven to 350°F. Put wings in a 9x12 casserole dish and coat with oil and ½ c. sauce. Bake for 25 minutes.

> ½ c. teriyaki sauce

Stir. Add remaining sauce. Bake another 20 minutes.

Original Source: The Kids Cookbook: Yum! I Eat it.

Turkey (Brined)

Brining is a very old way of preserving meat with salt.

> 14-16 lb. frozen turkey

Thaw turkey in the refrigerator for 2-3 days before beginning to cook and prepare the brine, below.

> 1 gallon vegetable stock
>
> 1 c. kosher salt
>
> ½ c. brown sugar
>
> 1 Tbsp. peppercorns
>
> 1½ tsp. grated ginger

Combine ingredients in a large stockpot over medium-high heat, stirring periodically until it boils. Allow to cool to room temperature and refrigerate until 12-24 hours before you plan to eat.

    1 gallon heavily iced water

    5 gallon bucket

Combine brine and ice water in the 5 gallon bucket. Remove the innards from the turkey and put it in the brine, breast side down. Weigh it down to keep it fully immersed, if needed, for the entire 8-16 hours it is stored in a cool place or refrigerated prior to cooking. Turn halfway through but ensure it remains fully immersed until you are ready to cook it.

Put the oven shelf on the lowest level and preheat the oven to 500°F. Remove turkey and dispose of the brine. Rinse turkey inside and out with cold water. Put a roasting rack inside a half sheet pan and put the bird on it. Pat dry.

    1 red apple, sliced

    1 c. water

    4 sprigs rosemary

    6 leaves sage

    Olive oil

Microwave the apple and water on high for five minutes. Add rosemary and sage and put it inside the turkey. Tuck wings underneath and coat the skin generously with olive oil.

Roast the turkey at 500°F for 30 minutes. Remove turkey and stick a probe thermometer into the thickest part of the breast. Reduce the temperate to 350°F and return it to the oven. In 2-2½ hours, it should be cooked to 161°F. (If the thermometer has an alarm, use it.) Loosely cover with foil and allow to rest for 15 minutes before carving. Use juices from the pan for gravy.

Original Source: FoodNetwork.com, courtesy of Alton Brown

Welsh Rarebit

This is simple: toast topped with cheddar cheese soup.

    1 can (8 oz.) Cheddar Cheese Soup

    ½ c. grated cheese

MAIN DISHES

1 Tbsp. Worchestershire or steak sauce
4 slices toast

Heat soup. Mix in cheese until it melts. Add sauce, if desired. Serve over toast.

15. Snacks

These are (generally) healthy, easy to make snacks. They may not be as healthy as a kale salad, but most of us (especially kids) don't really want to eat a kale salad. Compared to most of what kids love, peanut butter popcorn or curried nuts are the epitome of healthy eating. Several, such as dehydrated sweet and sour cucumbers, make great trail food.

If you want to make your own candy bars, the website "TheSpruceEats.com" has a collection of homemade candy bar recipes that is definitely worth checking out. It not only allows you to control the additives and decrease the sugar, but it means that as long as you have the ingredients, you can have treats that taste like Twix, peanut butter cups, and more of our favorites.

Tips for Melting/Dipping Chocolate

Coating sweets in chocolate creates a whole new treat, as anyone who has ever eaten a chocolate covered strawberry knows. Here are some tips for melting chocolate and dipping things in it.

- If you search for "candy decorating tools" the results should include inexpensive tools (less than $10 for some sets) for dipping things in chocolate. There are different tools depending on the shape and relative weight of what you are dipping.

- Since you need to use the chocolate as soon as it is melted, prepare everything else you need in advance.
- "Dipping chocolate" may require extra steps (tempering) but should give a better result than chocolate chips.
- Even a drop of water can cause melted chocolate to seize, becoming thick, grainy, and impossible to work with. Be careful to keep measuring cups, bowls, etc. dry as you are working with chocolate.
- To melt in the microwave, cook on 50%, not full power, to reduce the chance of burning it, for 15-20 seconds at a time, stirring before heating again to melt more lumps.
- To melt on a stovetop or campfire, heat to 118°F in a double boiler, testing temperature in the center of the chocolate for the most accurate reading.
- A little warmer is fine, but it can "seize" and get grainy if you aren't careful, especially in the microwave.
- If most of it has melted, stir the chocolate chunks so the rest of the chocolate can melt it.
- Place chocolate dipped items on parchment or wax paper to prevent/reduce sticking.
- Don't store chocolate in the fridge for more than a few days.
- Try the chocolate sauce or hot fudge recipe (Chapter 7).

Animal Cracker Cookies

These are really just another variation on rolled cookies, but they are tasty.

2½ c. flour

1 tsp. baking powder

½ tsp. salt

⅛ tsp. nutmeg

⅛ tsp. mace

Sift together over a small bowl.

>12 Tbsp. (1½ sticks) unsalted butter, room temperature
>
>1 c. sugar
>
>1 egg
>
>1tsp. vanilla

Beat butter until light and fluffy. Slowly add sugar and beat for two more minutes. Add egg and vanilla, and beat 1 more minute. Slowly add flour until it is all absorbed and dough starts to pull away from the sides. Divide into 2 equal part shaped like disks. Wrap in cling wrap and refrigerate from 2 hours up to 2 days.

Remove one disk and let stand at room temperature for 5 minutes. Place between two large, clean pieces of wax paper. Roll to ⅛" thickness. If rolling makes the dough crack, it's still too cold to roll out. Let it stand another 5-10 minutes at room temperature. Move rolled dough onto a floured surface and cut out shapes. If dough sticks, dip cookie cutters into flour then cut out shapes. Place on baking sheets lined with parchment paper. Refrigerate baking sheets with cookies for 30 minutes or freeze for 15 minutes. Preheat oven to 350°F. Bake cookies 14-16 minutes, until light golden brown. Move parchment sheets to wire racks to cool.

Candy Bar (Twix™-like)

This is a place chocolate dipping tools make life easier.

>1 batch shortbread cookie dough (page 179)

Preheat oven to 325°F. The easiest way to make shortbread for candy bars is to use small silicone molds such as ones for mini cupcakes or cookies. That allows you to fill them ⅔ full with cookie dough, leaving space to pour caramel on top after baking them. If you don't have a mold like that, you can press the dough into an ungreased pie pan or cookie sheet, or roll it flat and use cookie cutters. If cookies aren't in a bite-size mold, cut into the shape you want the final cookies. (The baked cookies are too hard to cut without crumbling if you skip this step.) Let cool completely while you start making the caramel.

1 batch caramel (page 52)

When the caramel is done, pour it over the finished shortbread. If you used a pan, fill to the edge with caramel. If you rolled and cut the cookies, pour enough to coat them. Put cookies in the freezer or refrigerator to cool and solidify.

½-1 lb. semisweet chocolate OR 1 batch chocolate sauce (page 51)

Melt chocolate, stirring every twenty to thirty seconds. Dip frozen bars into the melted chocolate, covering them completely, before putting them onto a parchment or wax-paper-lined tray. When all the bars are done, refrigerate for about ten minutes to set the chocolate. They will remain good for about one week.

Original Inspiration: TheSpruceEats.com (Make Your Own Twix Bars at Home) They have recipes for a lot of different candy bars.

Chips (potato, zucchini, or other vegetable)

Potato, zucchini, sweet potato

1 Tbsp. olive oil

Sea salt or flavored salt to taste

Pepper to taste

Preheat oven to at 450°F. Cut into thin slices. A mandolin slicer works well for this. Toss with remaining ingredients. Optional: top with other ingredients such as paprika, garlic powder, or whatever you enjoy. Bake 25 to 30 minutes, flipping halfway through.

I tried this with cucumber, potatoes, and baby carrots. The carrots came out as charcoal. On the other end of the spectrum, the cucumbers weren't crispy. The potatoes were just right but far better fresh. As they cooled, they lost crispness, which may be down to either needing cooked longer or coated with less olive oil since I used more than one tablespoon.

Curried Nuts

These giftable nuts are easy to customize to what you have.

1 Tbsp. butter

1 tsp. curry powder or other spice

1 c. whole nuts (salted is great)

Melt butter in a small skillet. Stir in the curry powder and add nuts. Sauté 1-2 minutes, until lightly browned. Scoop out onto paper towels to absorb extra oil.

GORP

This goes back to my days as a Girl Scout®.

Nuts

cereal (Cheerios™, Chex™, etc.)

Cheez-Its® or similar crackers

Dehydrated fruit or berries (including raisins)

M&Ms®

Chocolate chips

Other small, shelf-stable foods you enjoy

Dump them in a bowl, mix them, bag 'em, and go.

Granola Bar (Chewy)

This no-bake bar would be an ideal emergency snack. I made this with dried cherries because my dates had gone bad. It was good!

1½ c. (heaping) packed, pitted dates or other chewy, dried fruit

Chop dates in a strong food processor until it has a dough-like consistency, about 1 minute. (My small one didn't have enough power to do this.) Small bits will remain and it may form a ball.

1 c. roasted almonds, seeds, or other nuts, loosely chopped

1½ c. rolled oats

Optional Add-ins: chocolate chips, dried fruit

If desired, toast oats, seeds, and nuts (if raw) at 350°F until golden-brown, 10-15 minutes. Combine dates with oats and nuts.

¼ c. maple syrup, honey, or agave nectar

¼ c. creamy nut butter

Warm syrup and nut butter over low heat. Pour over date mixture, being sure to break up any clumps. Line an 8x8 baking dish with cling wrap or parchment paper to make removing the bars easier. Transfer mixture to the pan and cover with more cling wrap or parchment paper. Flatten to make the bars denser and hold together better. Firm in fridge or freezer for 15-20 minutes. Remove and cut into bars. Store in an airtight container.

Original Source: MinimalistBaker.com (Healthy 5 Ingredient Granola Bar)

Peanut Butter Buckeyes

These are so simple, but I really love peanut butter.

4 Tbsp. unsalted butter, melted

1 c. creamy peanut butter

2 c. confectioners' sugar

Combine and form into tablespoon size balls. Place on a parchment lined baking sheet. Freeze for 10 minutes.

6 oz. semi-sweet chocolate, melted

Partially dip each ball in the chocolate. Buckeyes normally have a peanut butter colored circle in the center of the chocolate, much like an eye. Return to baking sheet and refrigerate until firm, 25-35 minutes. You can also use the chocolate sauce receipt, although they will then need to stay in the refrigerator because of the low melting point.

Peanut Butter Popcorn

It sounds a bit odd, but oh my! Once I tried this, I was eating it by the fistful.

8 c. (2 qt.) popped, plain popcorn

Pop popcorn so it's done before the rest of the mixture.

½ c. sugar

½ s. corn syrup

Boil. Remove from heat.

½ c. chunky peanut butter

1 tsp. vanilla

Add to sugar mixture. Pour finished mix over popcorn.

Pumpkin Chocolate Chip Energy Balls

3 c. oatmeal

1 c. pumpkin puree

1 c. nut butter (peanut, almond, etc.)

⅔ c. maple syrup or raw honey

½ tsp. cinnamon

½ tsp. pumpkin pie spice

½ tsp. vanilla

4-6 Tbsp. ground flax seed

1 c. chopped nuts

½ c. mini chocolate chips

Combine. Roll into 1" balls. (An ice cream scoop is a good tool for this.) Put on sheet covered with parchment paper or a silpat and freeze 1 hour. Refrigerate until eaten, up to 1 week.

Original Source: CleanFoodCrush.com (Pumpkin Energy Balls)

Rice Cakes

Yes, they are bland, especially without any optional ingredients, but they are also easy to digest.

1 c. rice, uncooked

Preheat oven to 350°F. Grind in a blender or food processor.

1½ c. water

2 eggs

2 Tbsp. flour

Combine with ground rice. Grease a pan (donut, muffin, etc.). Bake 40-50 minutes. Tops will be brown. Sides will be crispy.

Optional ingredients:

> 2 tsp. parmesan cheese + 1 tsp. salt and pepper
> 2-3 tsp. sugar + 1 tsp. cinnamon

Add sweet or savory ingredients to rice cakes before baking.

Roasted Chickpeas

These are a tasty snack but they are also great on salads or pasta, or in soup. VeganHeaven.org has some great variations, like rosemary lemon and sweet roasted chickpeas. You can change this a lot just by using different spices or herbs.

> 2 cans (3 c.) chickpeas
> 2 Tbsp. olive oil

Preheat oven to 350°F. Rinse and drain canned chickpeas. Dry by rolling them in a clean dishtowel or paper towel. Toss with olive oil. Line a baking sheet with parchment paper, then spread chickpeas on it. Bake 25 minutes.

> 1 tsp. paprika
> 1 tsp. garlic powder
> ½ tsp. salt

Use these or any others you prefer–cinnamon, ginger, etc. Toss chickpeas with desired spices, ensuring chickpeas are evenly coated, then return to baking sheet. Bake an additional 10 minutes. Chickpeas will be brown and crunchy.

Original Source: VeganHeaven.org (Roasted Chickpeas)

Sweet and Sour Cucumbers

The sugar makes this a great quick-energy snack, especially dehydrated. The vinegar ensures it stays good for much longer than usual. This is my go-to snack for hiking because dehydrated sweet and sour cucumbers are light-weight, don't spoil quickly, and pack a much-needed sugar jolt.

    1 c. sugar

    1 c. vinegar

    1 c. water

Combine.

    4 cucumbers, peeled and sliced

Add cucumbers. Refrigerate 1 hour before eating or dehydrating.

Original Source: My Mother-In-Law

16. Desserts

Discussions of emergency food preparedness rarely include much discussion of desserts. Personally, I don't want to go a long time with no desserts any more than I want to go indefinitely with nothing to drink but plain water, much as I do enjoy water. This chapter has a wide variety of different desserts, including one recipe written for a Wonderbag.

Baked Cake Donuts

> 2 c. cake flour, sifted
>
> ¾ c. sugar
>
> 2 tsp. baking powder
>
> ¼ tsp. nutmeg
>
> 1 tsp. salt
>
> ¼ c. buttermilk
>
> 2 eggs
>
> 2 Tbsp. butter

Preheat oven to 425°F. Grease doughnut pan. Lightly beat eggs and melt butter. Combine dry ingredients and mix until just combined. Mix in remaining ingredients. Fill each cup half full (2 Tbsp. batter). Bake 4-5 minutes, until top springs back when touched. Cool in pan for 3 minutes, then remove. Top, if desired.

Brownies

My sons learned to make box-mix brownies in elementary school be-cause if they made them, then they could eat them. This really ups the game, though. If you have the time, I really recommend taking the time to go online and read the original recipe. She gives great expla-nations for how each step makes a difference.

> 12 Tbsp. unsalted butter, cut into 12 equal pats (1½ sticks)
>
> ½ c. chocolate chips or baking chocolate

Combine butter and chocolate in a microwave safe bowl. Microwave 15-20 seconds, then stir. Repeat until completely combined.

> ½ c. unsweetened cocoa powder
>
> ½ tsp. instant coffee grounds (optional)

Add to mixture and stir well.

> ¾ c. sugar
>
> ¾ c. light brown sugar

Add to mixture and stir well.

> 2 eggs + 1 egg yolk

One at a time, add eggs to mixture and stir well, at least 30 seconds per egg. This makes the brownie tops cracklier.

> 1 tsp. vanilla

Add to mixture and stir well.

> ½ tsp. salt

Sprinkle over mixture and stir well.

> 1 c. flour

Add to mixture and stir well.

> ¾ c. chocolate chips

Add to mixture and stir well. Pour into greased or parchment-lined 9x9 or 13x9 pan. Refrigerate for 15 minutes to 24 hours for cracklier tops.

Preheat oven to 350°F. Bake 30-35 minutes. Toothpick should come out fudgy but not covered with batter. Cool before cutting.

Original Source: SugarSpun.com (Brownies from Scratch)

Buttercream Frosting/Sugar Bombs

Kids love frosting enough to eat the frosting and toss the rest of the cake or cupcake. This sounds insane, but one Sugar Bomb is actually less sugar and less mess than a cupcake. This basic recipe is also a great base to experiment from. I added candy canes but cocoa powder, extracts, maple syrup, peanut butter powder, and more can be added for variety.

> ½ c. solid vegetable shortening
>
> ½ c. butter
>
> 1 tsp. vanilla
>
> 4 c. (1 lb.) confectioner's sugar
>
> 2 Tbsp. milk

Cream butter and shortening. Add vanilla. Gradually add confectioner's sugar until everything is mixed, scraping to ensure everything on the bottom and sides is mixed in. It will seem dry, so add milk and beat until light and fluffy. Add food coloring designed for frosting or use it white. If you need frosting, it's ready to use.

For sugar bombs, fill silicone ice cube trays and freeze. Pop out one frozen "sugar bomb" at a time. They melt quickly, so eat them soon after removing them from the freezer.

Candy Cane Buttercream Frosting

> 3 Tbsp. ground candy canes (to taste)

Add to buttercream frosting.

Candy Cane Shortbread Cookies

My family loves the plain shortbread cookies. One Christmas, we ended up with masses of broken candy canes and I started to experiment. I was concerned the peppermint taste might be overpowering but it is actually quite light.

> 3 Tbsp. ground candy canes
>
> 1¼ c. flour
>
> ½ c. butter (no substitutions)

Preheat oven to 325°F. Mix dry ingredients. Cut in the butter until well mixed and fine crumbs form. Knead until smooth. Pat or roll dough into your desired shape but it shouldn't be more than ½" thick. You can press the dough into an ungreased pie pan or cookie sheet, or roll it flat and use cookie cutters. Before cooking, cut into the shape you want the final cookies. (The baked cookies are too hard to cut without crumbling if you skip this step.) If desired, use your fingers to scallop the edges. Bake 25-30 minutes. Cut shapes again after removing from the oven, then cool for 5 minutes before transferring to a wire rack to finish cooling.

OPTIONAL: Add spices such as cinnamon, cloves, ginger, lemon peel, or poppy seed. Add sprinkles for special events.

PLAIN SHORTBREAD: Use 3 Tbsp. granulated sugar instead of 3 Tbsp. ground candy canes.

CARAMEL SHORTBREAD: Make the caramel recipe while the shortbread bakes. When the shortbread comes out of the oven, pour the caramel over it and cool. Sprinkle with coarse sea salt or flavored salt, if you like salted caramel.

Original Source: BH&G *Christmas Cookies* magazine 1998

Cheesecake

I like cinnamon graham crackers in the crust the best, but chocolate graham crackers would be good too. If you aren't a fan of graham crackers, the Vanilla Wafer Crust (pg. 203) is quite tasty.

> 15 crushed graham crackers*
>
> 2 Tbsp. melted butter
>
> 4 (8 oz.) packages cream cheese

1½ c. sugar

¾ c. milk

4 eggs

8 oz. sour cream

1 Tbsp. vanilla

¼ c. flour

*15 graham crackers is one cracker short of two packages, and one box generally contains three packages.

Preheat oven to 350°F. Mix crushed graham crackers and melted butter, then press into the bottom of a greased a 9" springform pan. Mix cream cheese and sugar until smooth. Add milk, then one egg at a time. Don't overmix. Add sour cream, vanilla, and flour and mix until smooth. Pour onto the pie crust and bake for 1 hour. Turn off the oven but keep the door closed while the cheesecake cools in the oven for 5-6 hours. (Cooling in the oven prevents, or at least reduces, cracking.) Refrigerate. Add toppings, if desired. Berry compote makes a great cheesecake topping.

Original Source: AllRecipes.com (Chantal's New York Cheesecake)

Chia Pudding

This is made of shelf-stable ingredients and provides fiber. Win!

2 c. milk (or 1 can coconut milk)

½ c. chia seeds

½ tsp. vanilla

Whisk the milk and vanilla together. When they are thoroughly mixed, whisk the chia seeds in and refrigerate for at least two hours to fully set. It is best eaten within a few days.

Optional Ingredients:

¼ c. maple syrup

1 Tbsp. honey

½ c. fresh blueberries or blackberries

¼ c. granola

Since this can be quite bland, it is a great recipe to personalize with seasonings (cardamom, cinnamon, extract flavorings) and add-ins (fresh or dried berries, granola) that you enjoy.

Chocolate Chip Cookies

Nestle puts THE chocolate chip cookie recipe on the back of the bag. Just cut the recipe off the bag. There is no need for another recipe or for any changes (other than, obviously, skipping nuts).

Original Source: Nestle

Chocolate Chip Peanut Butter Cookies

If you are running short on eggs (and just about everything else except butter), this is a great, easy treat. The optional ingredients take these from a simple brown sugar cookie to another level.

> ¾ c. packed brown sugar
>
> 1 c. butter, softened
>
> 1 egg yolk
>
> 2 c. flour

Optional Ingredients:

> 2 Tbsp. peanut powder + 1 Tbsp. water
>
> ¼ c. chocolate chips

Cream sugar and butter until light and fluffy. Add egg yolk, then flour and remaining ingredients. Refrigerate for 1 hour. Preheat oven to 325°F. Form into 1" balls and put on lightly greased baking sheet. Flatten and crisscross with fork. Bake 12-14 minutes.

Original Source: Cooking with 4 Ingredients

Cinnamon-Sugar Tortilla Strips

> 1 c. sugar
>
> 1 Tbsp. ground cinnamon
>
> 4 burrito-size flour tortillas
>
> ¼ c. vegetable oil

Preheat oven to 350°F. Combine cinnamon, sugar, and salt in a bowl. Brush both sides of the tortillas with vegetable oil and sprinkle cinnamon sugar mix on both sides. Cut into one inch strips and arrange on baking sheets, taking care not to overlap them. Bake for 20 to 25 minutes, flipping halfway through. Finished strips will be golden and crispy.

Coconut-Cherry Chews

These are one of my absolute favorite holiday cookies. Sadly, no one else in my family likes coconut and I can no longer eat an entire batch by myself, so I don't make them anymore. But I still love them!

> 1½ c. flour
>
> 1 c. sugar
>
> ½ tsp. baking powder
>
> ⅔ tsp. salt
>
> ⅓ c. butter

Combine. Preheat oven to 375°F. Grease cookie sheets.

> 1 c. coconut
>
> 2 tsp. almond extract
>
> 1 egg

Add to mix. Shape dough into 1" balls.

> 1 egg white, beaten
>
> 1 tsp. water
>
> 1-1½ c. coconut
>
> Maraschino cherries, cut in half

Combine egg white and water to create an egg wash. Dip dough balls in egg wash, then roll in coconut. Place 2" apart on cookie sheet. Place a cherry half in the center of each cookie and lightly press down. Bake for 11-14 minutes or until edges are light golden brown.

Cookie Pie Crust

I went looking for this when I wanted a cheesecake but didn't have any graham crackers on hand. I saw a box of these cookies, remembered making muffin size cheesecakes on them, and decided I needed to hunt down a recipe for a vanilla wafer crust. Enjoy!

> 1 box vanilla wafer OR ginger snap OR Oreo cookies
>
> ½ c. salted butter
>
> ¼ c. sugar

Melt butter. Smash cookies. You can use a mortar and pestle or put cookies in a baggie and use a rolling pin. Combine ingredients. Press into the bottom of a pan and top with cheesecake or pie ingredients. Bake following those instructions. For no-bake pies, refrigerate for 30 minutes or freeze for 15 minutes to set OR bake at 350°F for 10 minutes for a crispier crust.

Five Cup Salad

This is one way to get the kids to eat fruit! And it's a great last-minute pot-luck item.

> 1 c. pineapple chunks
>
> 1 c. mandarin oranges
>
> 1 c. miniature marshmallows
>
> 1 c. coconut
>
> 1 c. sour cream

Drain fruit. Combine. Chill.

German Crumb Cake

> ½ lb. butter
>
> 4 c. flour
>
> 1 egg
>
> 1 pinch salt
>
> 1 c. sugar
>
> 1 tsp. baking powder
>
> 1 tsp. vanilla

DESSERTS

Combine. Crumbs should form when you rub the dough with your hands. Press half the mixture into a greased 9" Springform pan.

> 1 Tbsp. breadcrumbs

Sprinkle on the dough

> 3 c. raw or canned fruit (apples, cherries, plums, etc.)*
> 1 tsp. vanilla
> Sugar to taste
> *Add 1 Tbsp. cornstarch to 2 cans canned fruit.

Preheat oven to 375°F. Cut raw fruit into pieces. Sprinkle canned fruit with cornstarch and cook for 2 minutes. Spread on the dough in the pan. Top with remaining dough. Bake for 40 minutes. Brush top with 1 Tbsp. of butter and sprinkle 1½ Tbsp. of sugar on top, if desired. Allow cake to cool and firm before removing the outer ring from the pan.

Original Source: handout in high school German class (true story)

Maple Cream Pie

I'm a huge fan of maple syrup, so when I found this recipe I just had to try it.

> 1 refrigerated pie crust

Press into a pie pan. Fill with dried beans or pie weights. Bake following package instructions. You want the shell to end up slightly browned. Remove weights to be sure the bottom is fully cooked as well, then cool crust in pan for 30 minutes.

> 2 packages instant vanilla pudding
> 2 c. whole milk
> 1 c. maple syrup

Whisk together. When well combined, pour into pie shell and refrigerate to set.

Optional Ingredients:

> Whipped cream

Maple Syrup

Serve topped with whipped cream and maple syrup.

Original Source: LazyGastronome.com (Vermont Maple Cream Pie)

Mousse in a Minute

Sometimes simple is best, and kids can even make this themselves, with a little oversight to be sure the lids really are on tight.

1½ c. cold milk

1 package instant pudding (any flavor)

Combine in a container with a tight-fitting lid. Shake vigorously for 45 seconds.

1 c. whipped topping

Add to mix. Reseal container and shake 15 seconds. Spoon into dessert dishes or refrigerate.

Peanut Butter Fudge

In third grade, the teachers decided we should learn basic cooking. We made one recipe every month for the school year, including this one. I love it. So does everyone else who tries it and survives the sugar shock. Diabetics should avoid this fudge at all costs!!

1 lb. butter

1 lb. peanut butter

2 lbs. confectioners' sugar

Optional Ingredients:

4 Tbsp. cocoa powder

Melt the butter. Mix in the peanut butter. Mix in the sugar and cocoa powder. You can also swirl the cocoa powder instead of fully mixing it for a different effect. It melts *very* easily, so try to keep this fudge refrigerated in the summer.

Peanut Butter Pie

I decided to swap out a Berry Pie in this cookbook for a cream pie. I went down quite the internet rabbit hole!!! I barely stopped at four new pie recipes and a crust. Now I have to force myself to make them all! My poor family, forced to endure more homemade desserts. (They may not get much peanut butter pie; it's one of my favorites.)

>   1 pie crust

Bake the crust in advance because it needs to be completely cool before being filled.

>   8 oz. cream cheese
>   1 c. smooth peanut butter
>   ¾ c. confectioner's sugar

Mix until light and fluffy

>   1 c. heavy whipping cream
>   ¾ c. confectioner's sugar

Combine cream and sugar until peaks form. Fold carefully into peanut butter mixture. Add filling to cool pie crust. Smooth top of filling. Freeze for 1 hour or refrigerate for at least 6 hours. Top with peanut butter cups, crushed cookies, chocolate chips, chocolate sauce etc.

Original Source: RecipesFromAPantry.com (No Bake Peanut Butter Pie)

Shoofly Pie 1

The first time I made shoofly pie, I didn't think it would work at all because the filling was completely liquid. I was sure I had missed flour to make the filling more solid. I was wrong. The filling really is straight-up liquid. The crumbs to sprinkle in the middle and on top, on the other hand, do need flour, and that's the cup of flour I missed the first time. Much better with all the ingredients!

>   Pie crust (purchased or from scratch)

Bake pie crust following the recipe. Cool to room temperature, or even in the refrigerator.

> 1 c. flour
>
> ½ c. brown sugar
>
> ¼ c. vegetable shortening, cold

Put the shelf on the bottom oven rack and preheat oven to 400°F. Combine flour and brown sugar. Use a pastry blender or your hands to cut in the shortening until small crumbs form. Set aside.

> 1 c. hot water
>
> 1 tsp. cornstarch

Dissolve corn starch into water. Set aside.

> ½ c. molasses
>
> ½ c. light corn syrup
>
> ½ c. brown sugar
>
> 2 eggs, lightly beaten

Combine. Add corn starch mixture and mix well. Pour half of the liquid into the pie crust. Sprinkle half the crumb mixture over it. Repeat with remaining mixture and crumb mixture. Bake on the bottom rack for 10 minutes at 400°F, then decrease temperature to 350°F. Bake for another 45-50 minutes. Remove and cool on a rack.

Original Source: DearCrissy.com (Shoofly Pie)

Shoofly Pie 2

I hesitated to include two versions of the same pie, but this is such a good one to use when the cupboard is bare that I went ahead because they use different ingredients to create the same pie. Just as with the first version, the uncooked filling is straight-up liquid.

> Pie crust (purchased or from scratch)

Bake pie crust following the recipe. Cool to room temperature, or even in the refrigerator.

> 1¼ c. flour

½ c. sugar

1 tsp. cinnamon

½-1 tsp. nutmeg

Pinch salt (unless you use salted butter)

½ c. butter

Preheat oven to 425°F. Combine spices. Cut in butter until mixture forms crumbs.

¾ c. warm water

¾ c. molasses (unsulfured not blackstrap)*

*Blackstrap is more bitter so if you only have blackstrap, substitute 2 spoonfuls of maple syrup for the blackstrap.

Heat water in a sauce pan, being sure not to boil. Remove from heat and stir in molasses.

½ tsp. baking soda

When molasses and water are fully combined, stir in baking soda. The baking soda and acid in the molasses will react. If it sets too long, the filling will be flatter. Pour into pie shell. Top with crumb mixture, paying extra attention to the edges. Bake 15 minutes, then reduce temperature to 350°F and bake another 35 minutes. Insert a knife in the center; it should come out clean.

Original Source: OurHeritageofHealth.com (Traditional Shoofly Pie)

Snow Cream

This can be made with shaved ice or snow. If you use snow, put a clean bowl out to catch fresh snow. If you live in an area prone to smog or dirty air, wait until enough has have fallen that it's clean before you start collecting snow to eat.

1 c. milk OR 1 can (14 oz.) condensed milk

1 tsp. vanilla

⅓ c. sugar

8 c. clean snow OR shaved ice

Combine all ingredients except snow. You can add a few drops of flavored extract, sprinkles, or even cocoa powder. Gradually add snow. If it's not thick enough, add more snow. Eat before it melts!

Vanilla Pudding

⅓ c. sugar

2 Tbsp. cornstarch

Pinch salt

2 c. milk

In 2-quart saucepan, mix sugar, cornstarch and salt. Gradually stir in milk. Cook over medium heat, stirring constantly, until mixture thickens and boils. (When the top is covered with small bubbles, it's boiling; it doesn't have to reach a rolling boil.) Boil and stir 1 minute.

2 large egg yolks, slightly beaten

Gradually stir at least half of the hot mixture into egg yolks to temper it, then stir back into hot mixture in saucepan. Boil and stir 1 minute; remove from heat.

2 Tbsp. butter, softened

2 tsp. vanilla

Stir in butter and vanilla. Pour pudding into dessert dishes. Cover and refrigerate 1 hour or until chilled. Store covered in refrigerator.

Vanilla Wafers

My goal with this cookbook is to make sure readers can make everything in here using shelf-stable ingredients. Store-bought cookies go bad far too quickly to be considered shelf-stable, and most of us eat them far too quickly for them to be part of our long-term storage.

Vanilla wafers are a good treat by themselves, but they are also a key ingredient in vanilla wafer pie crust, and something it never occurred to me to try to make at home – until I started this cookbook. They are really tasty and disappear super-fast! They haven't lasted long enough to make it into a pie crust yet, but I'm sure they will be fabulous. I hope your family enjoys these as much as my family does.

½ c. butter, softened

½ c. powdered sugar

¼ c. sugar

Combine and beat until pale and fluffy, 3-5 minutes on medium.

¼ c. milk

1½ tsp. vanilla

1¼ c. flour

½ tsp. salt

Preheat oven to 350°F Line baking sheets with parchment paper. Add milk and vanilla. When well combined, add flour and salt but don't overwork. Put dough in a pastry bag. If you don't have a 1A tip to use, just make sure you use a larger tip or cut a small, but not tiny, hole in the bag. Pipe 1" circles on baking sheets. Bake 20-24 minutes. Bottoms and edges will be golden brown.

Original Source: BakingAMoment.com (Homemade Vanilla Wafers)

White Cake

This simple white cake uses common long-term storage foods. The original name for the recipe is "Cold Water White Cake" and the basic cake is incredibly plain, which makes it a good base to experiment with. I want to try adding peanut butter powder and cocoa powder to jazz it up a bit.

4 egg whites

2 Tbsp. baking powder

Preheat oven to 350°F. Combine and beat until stiff peaks form.

2 c. sugar

½ c. butter

Cream sugar and butter together.

1 c. cold water

1 tsp. vanilla

2½ c. flour

Pinch of salt

Add to creamed sugar. Gently fold in egg whites. Grease and flour 9" cake pans. Bake 35-40 minutes.

Original Source: Amish365.com (Cold Water White Cake)

17. (Bonus) Sick-Day Recipes

This year, I came down with the flu Monday, our youngest son Tuesday, and our eldest Wednesday. It was a rough week and one where meals-as-usual definitely weren't cutting it just when I was way too sick to go out or even move much. (My beloved husband took each boy to the doctor and picked up prescriptions for all of us.) That led me to create this chapter focused on what you really need when you are sick, including non-edibles (hand sanitizer), rehydration solution in case you don't have Pedialiyte™ on hand, and homemade cough syrup.

One of the recipes I cut from this book was for rice porridge, Japanese sick people food. When that week hit, I tried it and is definitely a keeper for sick days. We keep instant boxes of flavored gelatin and pudding on hand, but what if you don't have any? Plain vanilla pudding isn't hard to make and neither is flavored gelatin, as long as you have milk and a gelling agent (gelatin or agar agar), respectively. And a recipe, of course.

I also wrote *Simple Cooking For Sick Days* which has these recipes and more arranged and changed as needed to make your life a little bit easier when you or someone you care for is sick. The first chapter is food for the first day, then drinks (tea, etc.). As you continue to feel better, continue through the chapters.

More Recipes In this Book

Rather than put move every recipe that is good when you are sick into this chapter, here is a list of good sick-day recipes from other chapters. Really, anything from the soup chapter and much of the bread chapter is good when you aren't feeling well, and so are many breakfast recipes.

Cough Syrup (Bourbon, for adults)

2 oz. bourbon whisky

2 oz. lemon juice (½ lemon, juiced)

1 Tbsp. honey

Optional Ingredients:

2-4 oz. water

Combine and heat all liquids except honey in the microwave for 45 seconds. Add honey and whisk. Microwave 45 more seconds. The ideal temperature is warm, not hot. For best effect, nurse it slowly.

Cough Syrup (Pineapple)

1 c. pineapple juice

¼ c. lemon juice

1 piece ginger (3")

1 Tbsp. raw honey

Optional Ingredients:

½ tsp. cayenne pepper

Combine. Drink ¼ c. 2-3 times per day until cough is gone.

Disinfecting Wipes

This and the hand sanitizer use essential oils, especially anti-bacterial ones. The best anti-bacterial essential oils include eucalyptus, lavender, oregano, peppermint, tea tree, and thyme. Each is best suited for specific things, so please do your research.

We use extra-thick paper towels in our house and I had to double the rest of the ingredients, so be aware that the "thirstiness" of your paper towels can impact how much you need to make.

Ziploc bags or other glass or disposable plastic container

18 paper towels or cloth squares

If the paper towels are larger than you want your wipes, cut them into the size you prefer. Put the towels in the sealable glass or plastic container. Metal can react to essential oils and plastic may absorb essential oils, many of which are not edible or even toxic. If you use a plastic container, don't use it for food storage in the future.

½ c. water

½ c. 70% rubbing alcohol

¼ tsp. liquid dish detergent (not the foaming kind)

4 drops tea tree, lavender, or lemon grass essential oil

Combine. Pour into the container. If it seals tightly, flip the container until the towels are fully saturated. Alternatively, shake it. The towels should absorb the liquid in about 30 minutes. If there is excess liquid, add more paper towels until it has been absorbed. If there isn't enough (as happened to me), make and add more.

DO NOT use near open flames!

Original Source: HouseWifeHowTos.com (Homemade Wipes)

Face Scrub (Coffee)

This isn't an obvious choice as a sick-day recipe but our hands and faces can need some extra scrubbing and why not use something that would otherwise be thrown out and helps moisturize?

> 1 tsp. honey
>
> ½ tsp. olive oil
>
> 1½ tsp. coffee grounds

Combine. Gently scrub your freshly-washed face. Wash off scrub; plain water is fine for this, no soap is needed.

Original Source: HeyItsLulu.blogspot.com (DIY Coffee Face Scrub)

Flavored Gelatin

Jell-O® brand flavored gelatin and saltines are two of the most basic sick-people foods. Box mixes of flavored gelatin are cheap, easy to make, and widely available. But if you don't like the available flavors or don't have any on hand, you can make your own.

I made this recipe using one package of Knox® unflavored Gelatin. Rather than 1 heaping Tbsp., it was short a bit of 1 Tbsp. The end result was still gelatin but it took longer to set up and was softer than regular gelatin.

> ½ c. juice
>
> 1 heaping Tbsp. gelatin

Pour juice over gelatin in a bowl. Whisk until well combined. Let "bloom" during the next step.

> 2 c. juice

Heat to a full boil. Pour over mixture that has been blooming. Whisk until completely dissolved. If you use tart juice (such as cranberry), you may need to add a small amount of sugar to taste or combine with a sweeter juice. Refrigerate 3 hours or until fully set.

(BONUS) SICK-DAY RECIPES

Original Source: LexisCleanKitchen.com (Homemade Jello)

Gelatin-like dessert (Agar Agar)

Gelatin isn't really very healthy so I sought out an alternative. Agar agar is extremely shelf-stable and healthy. Because agar agar is made from seaweed, this is also vegan-compliant. Win!

> 1½ tsp agar agar flakes OR ¾ tsp agar agar powder
>
> 1 c. juice
>
> 1 c. water
>
> ¼ c. sugar

Combine in a pot and bring to a boil, stirring regularly. Boil 2 minutes. If you use tart juice (e.g., cranberry), you may need to add a small amount of sugar to taste. Refrigerate 3 hours or until fully set.

Original Source: LovingItVegan.com (Fruity Vegan Jello)

Ginger Ale

Yes, you can make it at home!

> ½ c. honey
>
> ½ c. sliced, peeled ginger

Combine in a small saucepan. Simmer over medium for 15 minutes. Stir occasionally. Let cool. Pour cooled syrup through a fine mesh strainer, removing as much syrup as possible by pressing down.

> 4-5 c. club soda (approximately 1 liter)
>
> (Every time you pour club soda, you lose some carbonation so try to minimize pouring.)
>
> Fresh mint (optional)

Add to cooled, strained syrup. Stir and enjoy.

Ginger Ale #2

You can also make it without club soda, it just takes longer.

> 1½ oz. finely grated fresh ginger
>
> ¾ c. sugar

½ c. water

Combine in a small saucepan. Simmer over medium-high until sugar has dissolved. Cover and steep for 1 hour. Pour cooled syrup through a fine mesh strainer into a bowl. Remove as much juice as possible by pushing down on the mixture.

Ice

Water

You are making an ice bath for the syrup so the bowl you use for this step has to be large enough to hold the bowl with the syrup plus ice and water around it. Fill the bowl halfway with ice. Add enough cold water (hot water will melt the ice) to fill the bowl ¾ full. Put the syrup bowl over the ice bath, being sure the ice water doesn't overflow into the mixture. Keep uncovered. Let set until it reaches room temperature, refrigerating if needed. If it gets cold, it will be really thick.

7 c. water

⅛ tsp. active dry yeast

2 Tbsp. lemon juice

Pour syrup into 2 liter bottle. Add the remaining ingredients. You don't want a lot of extra room or the bubbles will dissipate too much. Gently shake to mix. After 48 hours at room temperature, open the bottle and check the amount of carbonation. Once you are happy with the amount of carbonation, refrigerate for up to 2 weeks, opening once a day to release extra carbonation.

Original Source: FoodNetwork.com (Ginger Ale)

Ginger Water

This is infused water, which is super simple to make.

½ tsp. of ginger or ¼" fresh thin-sliced ginger

4 c. water

You can clean and zest fresh ginger, or use some from the spice rack. Boil water. Add ginger and remove from heat. Steep 5 to 10 minutes, depending on desired strength. Remove and discard ginger. Drink hot or cold.

Hand Sanitizer

The aloe vera and vitamin E help keep your hands from drying out as much as they can with some other sanitizers. Instead of a spray bottle, I re-used an old pocket size hand sanitizer bottle. This has a lot of water, so it has a very low percentage of alcohol compared to many other hand sanitizers.

> 10 drops essential oil*
>
> 10 drops witch hazel, rubbing alcohol, or vodka
>
> 5 drops vitamin E
>
> 5 drops pure aloe vera (optional)
>
> *Common anti-bacterial essential oils include tea tree, citronella, eucalyptus, geranium, lemongrass, orange, patchouli, and peppermint.

Combine in a 2 oz. spray bottle. Shake to mix.

> Distilled/purified water

Add enough to fill the 2 oz. bottle. Shake before use.

Original Source: HopefulHolistic.com (DIY Hand Sanitizer)

Lip Scrub

This is one of the recipes I initially removed but put back. Why? When we are sick, our mouths can get germy, and they can also feel gross if we have been throwing up a lot. As with a facial scrub, a lip scrub can just make us feel better.

> 1 Tbsp. honey
>
> 1 tsp. olive or coconut oil
>
> 1 tsp. vitamin E
>
> 1 Tbsp. brown sugar

Combine ingredients. Apply to lips with a clean finger, scrubbing in circles. Rinse with lukewarm water. Add lip balm to lock in moisture.

Original Source: StyleCraze.com (DIY Lip Scrub)

Rehydration Solution

This isn't something that normally has a place in a cookbook but if you are sick, you need it, even when it isn't an emergency, and we all run out sometimes.

> 4 c. water
> ½ tsp. baking soda
> 3 Tbsp. honey or sugar
> ½ tsp. salt

Optional Ingredients:

> ½ packet unsweetened Kool-Aid

Mix everything together and serve. Refrigerate up to three days.

Rice Porridge (Okayu)

This is reputedly a common "sick-people food" in Japan. It should have 5 times more water than rice.

¼ c. uncooked short grain rice

Rinse the rice in water until the water runs clear. Soak rice in water for a minimum of 30 minutes, then drain.

1 c. water

Add water to the pot. Cook on low and for 40 minutes. Turn off heat and steam with the lid closed for another 10 minutes. Rice should be soft and thick.You can add a beaten egg (the hot rice will cook it), salt, salmon, sesame seeds, herbs, or anything else you want.

Original Source: JustOneCookbook.com (Rice Porridge Okayu)

18. Modifying Recipes

In an emergency, one of the biggest issues can be not having a key ingredient. Getting comfortable modifying recipes can be the key to handling that problem. Start experimenting now, while the stakes are low, so you are comfortable if you are ever in an emergency situation.

Look to other cultures to expand your options. If nothing else, it helps us all to see new options. I have found that Amish recipes and old cookbooks help me find simpler recipes that use fewer ingredients, more shelf-stable (long-term) ingredients, and are true basics, like how to make brown sugar. Asian recipes have helped me find ways to use leftovers and more rice-based recipes, which is great since rice stores so very well. Italian recipes clearly use a lot of pasta, which both stores well and is something you can make from scratch. On top of specifics like those, every culture has its own comfort foods. I had never eaten matzo ball soup before I added it to my cookbook but now I love it. It's also easy to make with long-term storage food.

Simplify, simplify, simplify. The fewer ingredients, the less chance you will run out of something. For example, many recipes call for several kinds of cheese. Substitute one young cheese that you can make for others that you don't have. (Young cheeses are ones that haven't been aged, which is another way of saying you can use them very soon after you start making them, like cream cheese or goat cheese.)

Substitute. You can often substitute honey for sugar. Stuffing with bread is a Thanksgiving standard but you can also make it with Matzo crackers. I substitute ginger for garlic in a lot of recipes. When I had ⅓ c. of light corn syrup and needed twice that amount for a shoofly pie, I used dark corn syrup for the rest of it. (This particular pie relies on molasses form much of its flavor, which is a big part of why that worked.)

Reimagine it. Salsa is best known as a tomato-based food but there are other kinds, such as peach salsa, that can extend your options. Beets are…beets, but they can also be used as a sweetener in baked goods. Ramen noodles can be a burger bun. Many things that are normally fried can be baked or even steamed instead, depending on what they are. Beer bread can be made with soda or selzer water instead.

Experiment with your family favorites to find new ways to use them right now.

Remove it. Spices are easy to remove from recipes. I make onion-free salsa. It is often surprisingly easy to remove ingredients from recipes, although that is less true of baked goods. Hopefully it is pretty clear why knowing what you can (and can't) remove is good in an emergency.

Change the condiments/sauce. Simply using olive oil or a different sauce (white, pesto) can change a meal entirely, helping to minimize boredom with a skimpy pantry. Something simple like infusing olive oil with herbs

Minimize it. There are many recipes where you can decrease the amount used for some ingredients. For example, if a recipe calls for four different spices, cut one, two, or even three. Every little bit helps when the cupboard is getting bare!

Add something: Spices can be your friend. Use them to make a bland diet more interesting or to change a meal entirely. The recipe for Ramen burger buns says to not use the spice packet, but you can add that spice to your burger itself or use it in the noodles to have a flavored bun to make a boring burger more interesting. If you have a garden, use some of the bounty to tweak a recipe.

Use what you have: One Christmas, I ended up with a whole bunch of candy canes my kids didn't want. I ground them up so they were about the same consistency as granulated (regular) sugar and started substituting them for sugar when I made deserts. In case you wondered, they are definitely good in brownies and shortbread. It would have been easier to just toss the broken candy canes, but this was a far better use of my resources and led to innovation on my part.

Combine things/use leftovers: The entire chapter on sushi is about ways to use leftovers. Play with it and come up with your own ideas for how to make sushi. Stir-fry is another great way to use leftovers and small amounts of food.

Appendix: Common Can Sizes and Equivalents

Can Size	Weight	Measurement
8 oz. can	8 oz.	1 cup
12 oz. vacuum	12 oz.	1½ cups
#1	11 oz.	1 1/3 cups
#2	1 lb. 4 oz. OR	2½ cups
	1 pint 2 fluid oz.	
#3		4 cups
#5	56 oz.	7 to 7 1/3 cups
#10	6 lb. 6 oz.	12 to 12 3/4 cups
condensed milk	15 oz.	1 1/3 cups
evaporated milk	6 oz.	2/3 cups
evaporated milk	14 1/2 oz.	1 2/3 cups
frozen juice concentrate	6 oz.	3/4 cup

Index

About the Author

Bethanne Kim was allergy free for most of her life, until she wasn't. She went to the allergist after onions started making her nauseous and was shocked to learn that she was highly allergic to most of nature and had allergy-induced asthma that was raging completely and utterly out of control. (In retrospect, that did explain the difficulty she had been having breathing.) On one test, she had the worst score her allergist had ever seen.

Like most people, this led her to learning more about allergies and taking a lot of medications. She's not the only one in her family with allergies. Thanksgiving is a particular challenge with the need to avoid wheat, corn, nuts, and more for the extended family.

She's a wife and the mother of two. Like too many families, cooking for everyone's dietary issues can be a challenge.

Other Books

The Constitution: It's the OS for the US explains the historical context for the US Constitution and describes how it works using computer terms like firewall and plug-ins, not legalese. (An OS is a computer Operating System, like iOS for Apple devices.)

Survival Skills for All Ages Book 1: Basic Life Skills covers skills so simple most emergency preparedness books skip right over them. In true emergencies, knowing how to sharpen kitchen knives and basic sanitation can be literal life savers. Skills were chosen for their value in everyday life as well as emergencies.

Survival Skills for All Ages Book 2: 26 Mental & Urban Life Skills covers financial skills, staying safe while traveling, self-defense, cyber security, hiding from danger, handling your emotions (including stress and anger), and more. These skills can help kids and adults throughout life, not just in emergencies.

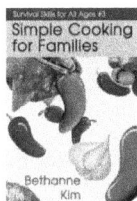

Survival Skills for All Ages Book 3: Simple Cooking for Families is full of simple recipes that can be cooked with long-term storage ingredients and basic farm produce (dairy and eggs), and recipes for staples such as baking powder, sweetened condensed milk, and crackers. It also talks about the tools you need to cook without power.

OTHER BOOKS

Survival Skills for All Ages Book 4: Simple Cooking for Allergies: Oral Allergy Syndrome and Low Histamine Food explains what foods are low histamine, why others are high histamine, and how to eat a low histamine diet while also avoiding the uncooked fruits and veggies that can cause problems for OAS sufferers.

Cubmastering: Getting Started as Cubmaster is an introduction for new Cubmasters. Topics covered include organizational structure, training, recruiting, and recharter. This is about more than just the nuts and bolts of Scouting, though. It also covers dealing with difficult parents and planning special pack events.

Scout Leader: An Introduction to Boy Scouts focuses on the nuts and bolts of the Boy Scouts of America with particular emphasis on how units in Cub Scouts and Scouts BSA are supposed to work. Recharter, training, common meetings (Roundtable), and much more are described. Each chapter starts with a quote from Lord Baden Powell.

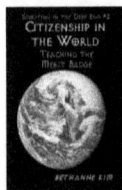

Citizenship in the World: Teaching the Merit Badge is, quite simply, a guide to assist merit badge counselors in teaching the BSA Eagle-required merit badge "Citizenship in the World." It includes the merit badge requirements, and information and tips for teaching it.

The Organized Wedding: Planning Everything from Your Engagement to Your Marriage is chock full of checklists. No detail is too small! What truly sets it apart is including the actual wedding ceremony and a chapter on your marriage with questions on financial priorities, family health history, and all your doctors.

OMG! Not the Zombies! Book 1 A group of teens goes for a hike and accidentally starts the zombie apocalypse. Being good at being prepared, they start setting up a safe community in the old Indian cliff houses and stocking it with supplies to save themselves and their families while the adults are still pretending life is normal.

BRB! Not the Zombies! Book 2 As their group grows, they discover a new mission: Get crucial information and items to the CDC to help with efforts to create a cure for the Infection. They fight their way through zombie-infested towns and to find the "impregnable" CDC research station their hopes are pinned on.

YOLO! Not the Zombies! Book 3 Have you ever wondered how a hurricane might affect the zompoc? Or how undead would fare in a sandstorm? (Hint: Hope they aren't wearing a helmet.) These and other natural disasters are explored in these zombie short stories.

Works in Progress:

Survival Skills for All Ages: 26 Outdoor Life Skills covers basic camping skills such as knot tying, fire building, outdoor cooking, and choosing a tent. It also covers hunting, fishing, and foraging for food; finding your way using maps, compasses, and GPSs; and truly basic skills such as managing time and water safety (tides, currents, etc.).

Survival Skills for All Ages: Special Needs Prepping may sound like something only "other people" need but the truth is that most families have special needs. Babies, elderly parents, diabetes, asthma, allergies–most of us have at least one of these and even if we don't, a simple sprained ankle or back injury can make us (temporarily) special needs.

Contact the Author

Bethanne Kim would love to hear from you! You can connect with her through:

Email: Bethanne@BethanneKim.com

Blog: BethanneKim.com

Facebook: BethanneKim

Pinterest: BethanneKim

Twitter: @Bethanne_Kim

Instagram: BethanneKim

Because Amazon reviews really do matter, especially for indie authors, please take a few minutes and post a review of this book on Amazon.com.

www.ingramcontent.com/pod-product-compliance
Lightning Source LLC
Chambersburg PA
CBHW071336090426
42738CB00012B/2918